FALL AGAIN, RISE AGAIN

FALL AGAIN, RISE AGAIN

SANDEEP AGGARWAL

with

SUNNY SEN

RUPA

Published by
Rupa Publications India Pvt. Ltd 2020
7/16, Ansari Road, Daryaganj
New Delhi 110002

Sales Centres:
Allahabad Bengaluru Chennai
Hyderabad Jaipur Kathmandu
Kolkata Mumbai

ISBN: 978-93-90356-39-3

Second impression 2021

10 9 8 7 6 5 4 3 2

Printed at Saurabh Printers Pvt. Ltd.

To my mother Savitri,
my father Raj Kumar Aggarwal and
my sons Ahaan and Arjit

CONTENTS

PROLOGUE

It was December 2013. I was down and out—a feeling that was not alien to me. However, this time around I didn't feel I had it in me to resurrect myself—yet again—and perhaps I was down for the count. The pain and hurt stemming from the crisis in my personal life and the legal case in the US had taken their toll. Sitting on the balcony of my house in Delhi, I stared aimlessly, somewhat despondently, at a stray kite that had appeared on the horizon.

I felt a tap on my shoulder. One of my closest friends, Vishesh Tandon, had just walked in. Sensing the storm that had built inside me, he said, 'I know you. You need to fly your kite once again. The winds are not favourable, so wait; but keep the kite and thread ready. Soon, with the right tailwind, you will be able to fly your kite higher than before.'

Vishesh knew me just too well and his words had the desired effect. I pulled myself out of the phase of self-pity and set myself on the path of another adventure—Droom—yet again.

1

YOU WILL FAIL!

'Your son doesn't know anything; I won't be surprised if he fails his exams,' one of the teachers at S.D. Model School told my father. I was in class four, but could neither spell a word in English nor was I good in other subjects.

I was nine at the time, and was both underconfident and reticent. Destiny had not been kind to me as I had been forced to attend yet another Hindi-medium school.

My kindergarten in Chandigarh had perhaps been the best school I had attended till then, mainly because the medium of instruction was English. That association ended as soon as my father's transferable job forced our family of six—my parents and three older siblings—to move every few years.

I was born in a government hospital in Chandigarh in 1972—a

time of scarcity, rationing of essential goods, unemployment and disenchantment; a time of songs like '*Haal chaal thik thak hai, Sab kuchh thik thak hai ... Kaam nahi hai varana yaha, Aap ki dua is sab thik thak hai* (I am fine, Everything is fine... There is no hope of getting a job. But with your blessings everything is fine).' I was the fourth child in the Aggarwal household. Raj Kumar and Savitri had two daughters, Reeta and Simpy, and a son, Raman, before me.

My father was an engineer with Haryana Public Works Department (PWD), the government arm that builds public infrastructure. Jobs were scarce and anyone with a government job was considered privileged, even though the salaries were meagre. We had moved into a small one-room rented flat in a lower-middle-class neighbourhood in Chandigarh soon after I was born. The size of the room didn't matter to me, for I was just a child.

I remember my father leaving early every morning and coming back late at night. He was a very simple and hardworking man with a kind and generous heart. He was a loving father and a dedicated husband. He made sure that positive social and family values were instilled in us.

Those were carefree days. I was four and followed my older brother Raman, who was twelve, everywhere. Raman was good at flying kites, and I was happy if I was just allowed by him to hold the string for a bit. I would often end up bruised while scaling walls and parapets that Raman scaled with ease. Injuries were routine. Everything seemed like an adventure. I felt like a big boy.

Kites continue to fascinate me even today, and now they even inspire me. Kites are fearless, bold and yet grounded. Kites understand the importance of lying low when the wind is too much or too little and soaring when the winds are favourable. I hope this philosophy will help make Droom India's most successful company, sooner rather than later.

GUHLA. WHAT IS THAT?

It was 1976. I had just started attending school in Chandigarh, when one evening my father came home and said, 'I have some good news and some bad. I have been promoted to the rank of a class one officer and transferred to Guhla.'

'Guhla?' my mother asked. She had never heard that name. Actually, neither had my father before that day.

All of us were gutted. Chandigarh was India's best-planned city and we loved living there. I was too young to understand the importance and meaning of a promotion, and I thought that it was some sort of punishment.

Guhla was around three hours from Chandigarh. Like most villages in the northern Indian state of Haryana, the infrastructure was abysmal—bad roads, hardly any schools or hospitals and intermittent power supply. The saving grace: my father was the highest ranked government officer in the village and got respect from everyone.

My father had the four of us admitted to the US equivalent of the public education system school—the Prathamik Sikhsha Kendra—the only school in the neighbouring three villages. The school was a 30-minute walk from our new, much bigger home. They taught in Hindi. Since many of the classes were held in the open, the four of us carried jute mats on which we sat. The school had no money to buy benches. The paucity of funds meant there was just one toilet, and it was reserved for the girls—200 of them. Boys had to go outside the school compound to answer the call of nature.

We started enjoying the new life—open spaces, playing outdoors, climbing trees and swimming in the ponds. Television was limited to the affluent lot those days and our only source of entertainment was the radio. I remember our entire family listening to 'Hawa Mahal' and Hindi songs on All India Radio while having dinner.

The radio was also our only source of news. One day we heard that Prime Minister Indira Gandhi had declared Emergency. Although the radio didn't tell us about it, we heard that anyone opposed to the establishment was being put behind bars.

On the other hand, India was making a mark globally. The Indian cricket team defeated the mighty West Indies, and Parveen Babi, the Bollywood sensation of the time, had been featured on the cover of *Time* magazine. Guhla remained the sleepy hamlet it was, untouched by whatever was happening in India.

The project for which my father was sent to Guhla—building metalled roads in and around the village—got over. The transfer orders to move from Guhla came in 1979, I think.

KALKA MAIL

Our next stop was Kalka, another small city in Haryana, and literally the last city on the plains before one began the ascend to the mighty Himalayas. By now my father was doing quite well in his job and we were allotted a bigger government accommodation than Guhla in Kalka. My mother was quite excited to move back to a town for two reasons—first, her children would get better education in an

English-medium school and, second, she loved the idea of a bigger accommodation. Luck failed us on both accounts.

After arriving in Kalka, my father was asked to move into a small government accommodation temporarily. This arrangement was a matter of a few days until the officer he was replacing moved out from the larger house. However, my father's predecessor, who had been transferred from Kalka, stalled the transfer using some political connections and didn't vacate the place. What followed was worse.

The presence of two equal ranked officers in the same town meant that my father was immediately transferred to Chandigarh.

My parents' attempts to get me into an English-medium school also failed. All the principals said, 'Your son does not know how to speak, read or write English. We can't admit him.'

I had to settle for a local government school in Kalka.

DAD ON WEEKENDS

My father joined his new office in Chandigarh, while we stayed back in Kalka. Chandigarh was 30 km from Kalka—a huge distance in those days because public transportation was in bad shape. He left early morning and returned late every night.

Kalka was a new town for us, but my father was hardly around. Those were times when women would barely step outside their houses without their husbands. Understandably, people found it shocking that a wife was managing everything single-handedly—kids' education, shopping, the house. Now, when I look back, I can imagine the kind of stress my parents were under, especially my mother. I, on the other hand, was too young to feel any stress, let alone theirs. It didn't even matter to me that I didn't get admitted into a good school, but it sure haunted me later in life.

The only thing I found strange was that my father didn't spend much time with us. It made me sad. This was perhaps my first brush with 'stress'; actually, 'distress'. My sisters and brother understood the reasons.

The weekends were great. I still remember my father taking us to the town's weekly Sunday market and buying us goodies. Our stay in Kalka was short, though. My father was again transferred to Karnal, another small town in Haryana, but much bigger than Guhla and Kalka.

THE PRICE OF LOVE

Within six months of moving to Karnal, my mother tried to teach me English, a language alien to her, too. She ended up asking me to read the English book prescribed by the school. But how? I barely recognized the alphabets.

In Karnal, too, I failed to get into an English-medium school. That is when I joined S.D. Model School. Due to the constant transfers, my studies were badly affected and I was one of the weakest students in my class. That was the time when the incident mentioned at the beginning of this chapter took place. One of my teachers told my father, 'I won't be surprised if he fails his exams.' What a terrible thing for a father to hear!

Reinforcements were called in—a private tutor. I was gifted a shining new bicycle by my father and I would ride it everyday to my tutor's home and back. I passed the exams.

The three-year cycle of transfers came yet again and my father was asked to relocate to Fatehabad, another small town that was near Haryana's border with the desert state of Rajasthan. Fatehabad was very far from my hometown Chandigarh.

We were allotted a temporary two-bedroom house in the government officers' colony. That's where I saw Zuby, my first crush. Her house was opposite ours. She was beautiful.

Few girls went to school in Fatehabad; Zubi did. She was smart and popular. We became friends.

I was twelve at the time. My friendship with Zubi didn't go down well with the neighbourhood boys—they stopped playing with me. Zubi's friendship came at a high price.

SAVE ME, MR COLOUR TV

One day in school I heard one of my classmates talking about the most amazing thing he'd seen till then—colour television. Wow!

A television was the ultimate status symbol among middle-class households, and a colour television made you part of the elite. Till that time we didn't own even a black and white television. Being the youngest child, I exploited my parents' affection and somehow coaxed and cajoled them to buy a colour television. The Dianora colour television not only helped my budding romance but also helped me patch up with my friends.

Here's how.

When we bought the television, there were long queues of people outside our house, just to catch a glimpse of it.

It was 1982. Only two other houses in the neighbourhood had television, but none of them were colour. The era of colour television coincided with the hosting of the Asian Games in Delhi.

The Games were flagged off on 19 November 1982 and so was colour television broadcast. During the Games, our house became a picnic spot. At times there was barely space to walk in the living room. I still remember how my mother made endless cups of tea and pakoras (fritters) for the guests. India did very well—won 57 medals, including 13 gold—and ranked fifth in the overall medals tally.

The kids who had boycotted me suddenly became friendly. They wanted to watch the Games as well as Hindi films shown on Sundays and foreign animation series like *Spider-Man* and *He Man*, which were quite popular in the early 1980s in India. Zubi, too, started spending more time at my place. We always watched *Spider-Man* together.

Every evening, some of the families from the neighbourhood would come to our house to watch *Hum Log*, a very famous Hindi TV serial of the time. This was the first time I realized that if you have something unique, something different, something that is not commonly available, people will flock around you.

Many years later, I built my startups around the same philosophy.

THE ABC OF FRIENDSHIP

The kids soon got bored of television. Moreover, owning a colour television was no more a novelty because many other households also bought it. Worse, Zubi's parents got transferred. I was alone once again.

I tried other ways to be part of the neighbourhood clique. Once I bought a new bat and offered it to them to play with. I even shared my other toys, but somehow none of that worked. I remained an outsider.

So I decided to make my own clique. Manoj Bajaj and Sanjay Chawla were in my class. We had a common love—badminton. We went on to play in the under-18 category at the district level.

Over the next year our friendship became almost legendary in school. We ate, played and studied together. Because of the initials of our last names—Aggarwal, Bajaj and Chawla—we were called the 'ABC' group.

FLATTENING THE GROUND

Back at school, we didn't have an indoor playing area; we just had a playground. Playing badminton in the open was tough and we constantly battled with both wind and sun.

So we requested the school to build an indoor arena. By the time the management decided to go ahead with the plan, I was in class X—a few months before I graduated from senior secondary.

We didn't want to miss an opportunity to play badminton, so we volunteered to help in building the indoor arena. The ABC group helped flatten the ground and even laid some of the bricks. It was a great feeling. The excitement of building something from scratch cannot be described in words.

The same happened when, against all odds, I built ShopClues as a virtual marketplace for people to shop online. It seems like yesterday that I made the first presentation, offered the first few products and made the first sale.

2

MINORITY REPORT

In comparison to today, when 65 per cent of women are literate, only 30 per cent had the opportunity to study at that time. However, one aspect has remained the same—girls continue to take education much more seriously than boys.

Ours was a co-educational school, but girls and boys were segregated in different sections. When I was in class eight I was among the brightest students in my class. When I got promoted to class nine, the unthinkable happened. The school's principal decided to move the best students from among the boys to the girls' section.

The girls were more serious about studies, so the principal thought they would be a good influence on the boys. There were seven of us in a class of 30 girls. It was mighty awkward in the beginning and remained so for the next two years that we spent in that class. We were made to sit on the backbenches. Awkwardness turned into embarrassment when the teachers scolded us.

Ritu was one of the girls in the class. She was beautiful, good in her studies and even better at sports. The teachers loved her, and so did all the boys.

Even before I could muster the courage to talk to her, my best friend Sanjay swept her off her feet. Ritu was tall and played badminton. Sanjay was taller and also played badminton. It was unfair. I played better badminton than Sanjay, but maybe I wasn't tall enough to catch her eye.

THE SCIENCE OF COMMERCE

I scored 70 per cent in class ten and ranked second in my school. Scoring 70 per cent wasn't as easy then as now. I know it might sound strange nowadays when even 98 per cent doesn't seem enough.

It was time to choose a stream for the next two years of my schooling. The choice was between science, commerce and arts. In my case the choice had supposedly been made, for two reasons. One, the moment anyone scored 70 per cent in those days, they were expected to take up science; and, two, my father was an engineer.

I stood up in defiance and took up commerce. My parents supported my decision wholeheartedly. All of us had seen how miserable my elder brother had been while studying science.

Raman tried hard to fulfil my father's dream of becoming an engineer. There was additional pressure from society—how could an engineer's son not study science?

He gave in to societal and parental pressures, even though he didn't want to. He passed class twelve, and then appeared for the engineering entrance exams. He failed all of them.

My father was crestfallen. Raman was mocked by outsiders. But he was tough and made it his mission to prove everyone wrong. He's the one person who made me believe that you don't need to be an engineer to become successful. He's now a well-respected chartered accountant as well as a successful real estate businessman. Raman and cricketer Yuvraj Singh co-own many real estate projects.

MY FOSTER PARENTS

Raman was like my foster father and my sister Reeta my foster mother. Being the youngest has its own perks—I was pampered to the hilt. Raman would often take the blame for my mischief and get punished by my father. I remember when Raman and his friends wanted to watch *Sholay*. My father was away from home for some official work. I pestered my brother to take me with him to see the film.

The cinema hall was at a distance, so we took a bus. I saw my father's jeep on the way. I shouted, 'Papa, papa.' He saw us and made us get off the bus. Raman was severely punished.

Raman moved to Chandigarh when I was in class nine. For the first time I was without him by my side. It wasn't easy.

GROWING UP

After my schooling, I joined Dyal Singh College in Karnal. I was in college for the next five years. In my fourth year, however, my father again got transferred to Bahadurgarh, a small town on the outskirts of New Delhi. My mother and Simpy moved with him. I stayed behind in Karnal for my education and rented a small room with another college mate.

I did very little those days other than aimlessly roaming around the city, drinking, chasing girls and playing badminton. Yes, that's all I did.

Naturally, I barely scraped through college. Raman came to know how useless and aimless I had become. He asked me to join as a trainee in his chartered accountancy firm. He even got me enrolled into the chartered accountant (CA) course. With no other job in sight, I joined Raman and started preparing for the CA exams. We did audits for banks like the State Bank of India and Canara Bank, among others.

During one of these audits, I had to go to the branch office of the government-owned HAFED, near Karnal. I travelled in an Ambassador car, packed in with seven other people. It was hot and humid. To make matters worse, one of the co-passengers started smoking a bidi (a form of Indian cigarette) inside the car. I still hate the smell of bidi. The branch was in shambles and the employees were openly hostile towards me. Clearly, they did not want anyone to audit their accounts. But I had a job to do, which I did and left.

I distinctly remember another audit, which was when I finally decided that this was not what I wanted to do in life. I was sent to audit a branch of the State Bank of Patiala in the Sirmour district of Himachal Pradesh. Bus service was limited—one bus took you there in the morning and the next bus brought you back. I took the bus all right, but ended up at the wrong place. It was a stunningly beautiful village, with the mountains on one side and the river Beas on the other. While I waited the next 4–5 hours for a bus, realization dawned that accounting was not for me; but more importantly, I promised myself that I would do something worthwhile in life. My family should be proud of my achievements. I took the next bus out of that place and bid goodbye to auditing.

Next stop: MBA.

RUNAWAY STUDENT

Once I had decided to quit accounting, I confided in my mother. I felt trapped, I told her, and she stepped in like a tigress and rescued me. She called one of her brothers, who was then a senior government officer in Mumbai (then Bombay), and asked him to help me. She spoke to my father and soon I moved to Mumbai. I started going to one of the best MBA coaching institutes there.

The institute's classes were held in St Xavier's College. It was a different world—students drove to the institute in their fancy cars, wore trendy clothes and spoke in impeccable English. By then, I was good at reading and writing in English, but was not confident speaking it. The very first day there was a nightmare for me—no English, no fancy clothes and no car.

The city of dreams had broken all my dreams in one day. I spent the next few days exploring the city, eating local food and finding reasons to return to parents.

DEATH OF A DREAM

Within a month, I returned to Chandigarh, but I was sure that I wanted to study business management.

I found, through acquaintances, that someone named Sandeep Mann ran Chandigarh's only management training institute—

Ekadhiken Niketan. It was just three years old, and had already scaled to 100 students that year. I was one of them.

Sandeep Mann was Raman's age, and later I came to know that both of them had studied together in Karnal. Sandeep became quite fond of me. I started spending more time at the coaching centre, even after my classes—reading English books and occasionally chatting with Sandeep. My English improved vastly during this time. But was it enough?

In the evening, we would walk up to the market to have a cup of tea, and grab some snacks.

He taught me new ways to combine mathematics and logical reasoning. Few of those tricks I would never forget. One day, he picked up a packet of Maggi noodles and spelt it: MAGGI. He looked at me and said, 'M = 12 (M is the twelfth alphabet) and A = 1 (A is the first). What is the total of all the alphabets?' In the next few months I became very good at such calculations, and could even beat Sandeep at this game, at times.

I thought I was ready to take the MBA entrance exams. I appeared in fourteen tests, but managed an interview call from only one institute—Bikaner University. Even there I got rejected because of my weak English.

That was 1991—an era when India changed as a country and my life as an individual also changed forever. This was the time when suicide bombers had assassinated Rajiv Gandhi and the Congress party had come back to power riding on a massive sympathy wave. By the time P.V. Narasimha Rao was sworn in as the prime minister, the country's economic growth was down to 1.1 per cent, and inflation had hit 17 per cent.

Manmohan Singh became the finance minister, and started what was called the 'Liberalization Era' and opened the gates for greater flow of foreign money into India. There was a ray of hope for the country.

But my failure in getting into Bikaner University had shattered me completely. No ray, no hope?

3

OPERATION BLUE STAR

It was October 1984 and Prime Minister Indira Gandhi had just been assassinated by her Sikh bodyguards as a revenge for Operation Blue Star.

Earlier that year in the month of June the Indian Army had entered the holiest shrines of the Sikhs—the Golden Temple in Amritsar—to flush out extremists led by Jarnail Singh Bhindranwale. Bhindranwale and his followers were fighting to create an independent Sikh state called Khalistan. By the time the Operation ended, hundreds of supporters of Khalistan, including Bhindranwale, as well as innocent civilians, had been killed. The Golden Temple was badly damaged and Sikhs across India and the world felt insulted and outraged at the high-handed approach adopted by Indira Gandhi.

I still remember the morning of 31 October. My parents woke me up early. We were to return to Fatehabad from Pushkar, where my parents, grandparents, Simpy and I had gone on a pilgrimage. It was a 12-hour drive back home. All of us packed ourselves into an Ambassador car that my father had hired.

'Why are the roads so deserted?' my father asked our Sikh driver. Even the motels and dhabas on the highways were shut. None of us knew of Indira Gandhi's assassination. Finally, we found a dhaba that was open, and we stopped for a cup of tea. The owner of the place told us about the assassination. The reports of anti-Sikh violence, in which thousands of innocent Sikhs were killed, started coming from different parts of north India following an announcement at 2.23 p.m. by doctors at Delhi's AIIMS hospital that Indira Gandhi was dead.

We were told that it was not safe to drive with a Sikh driver. Cars were being stopped and Sikhs were being pulled out and killed. I was too young to fully understand the seriousness of the situation, but I was very, very scared. The thought of people stopping our car, pulling out our 'driver uncle' and slaughtering him made me start crying.

For everyone's safety, the driver took off his turban, cut his hair and shaved his beard, so he couldn't be identified as a Sikh. We reached home very late in the night because of the frequent detours. It was the first time I realized that even ordinary people could go to the extent of killing other people when they were angry. Death became an immediate reality. Through all this, my father stayed calm. Many people we met along the way advised him to abandon the trip and stay put till the violence ended. He kept saying that we needed to overcome our fears to reach our destination. '*Aage badte rehna chahiye* (We should keep marching ahead),' he told us.

BIKES AND AVIATORS

Overcoming obstacles is difficult, but dealing with failure and rejection is the hardest. Barring one, each and every management institute I had applied to had rejected me. My only ray of hope has also faded when I failed to get into Bikaner University. But I reminded myself of what my father had said after Mrs Gandhi's assassination: 'We should keep going forward.' So, forward it had to be.

I turned to Sandeep Mann, yet again. He was happy to see me back at his institute. 'Let's work together and make this happen,' he said.

His words were inspiring. For the next one year, I gave it everything I could. I studied for seventeen to eighteen hours every day. I did not allow myself to relax and think I had completed the course and could crack the entrances this time. A fear of failure had taken hold of me, and it drove me forward relentlessly.

Finally, I wrote twenty entrance exams. I still couldn't crack the Common Aptitude Test (CAT), but that didn't disappoint me much. I got interview calls from universities in Pune, Mumbai, Delhi and a few other places as well. Devi Ahilya University, Indore, was the college I selected. In those days it ranked among the top ten universities to study MBA.

I had not only got through; I also managed to get a University Grants Commission (UGC) scholarship. That year 200 people took admission in the MBA programme and seven of us got the UGC scholarship. So I paid only Rs 400 per semester, while most of my batchmates paid up to a couple of lakh rupees. The UGC scholarship opened up other avenues for me. It was easy to secure a room in the hostel, thanks to the scholarship, though the rooms themselves were in a dismal condition.

At the time, I visited my brother Raman and told him about the condition of the hostels. Raman was well off—his business was doing well. He was appalled by what he heard. 'You are already saving so much money, thanks to the scholarship. There is no need to stay in a hostel. Take a room on rent. I will send you the money,' he said.

Indore was seeing something like a construction boom then and for the first time condominiums were being built for those who could afford them. I rented a two-bedroom flat in Hari Om Apartments, hoping to find a flatmate to share my expenses with. The move proved quite entrepreneurial. I found the flat I wanted to take on rent and signed the lease and bought mattresses for a second person who would share half the rent. Within a couple of weeks, a friend moved in.

My friends in Indore called me Sandy. I liked this name so much that I spray-painted the balcony with the words: Sandy's Den. I also bought a motorcycle, a Bajaj Kawasaki.

Within six to seven months I realized that owning a Bajaj Kawasaki wasn't sexy enough. I sold it and bought a Yamaha RX100, a bike that enjoyed cult status among the youth in those days, and continues to do so even now. That was not all. In December 1994, Ray-Ban launched its aviator sunglasses in India. I bought a pair for Rs 2,000, which was a big sum then. Getting the money for this purchase was not easy, though. Here is how I did it.

There was a hotel near our institute hostel, a place called Golden Palace. It was run by a Sikh family. One evening I walked into the hotel and introduced myself to the owner. I told him that I was a student of business management studies and I could analyse the market for him. I asked for Rs 3,000 to do the work. The man was fascinated by the idea and agreed to hire me to do market analysis and survey for him.

I did the survey and got the money from the satisfied customer. I spent Rs 2,000 on the sunglasses and started wearing them to college.

And it was in Indore, a year after I arrived, that I met a beautiful girl named Radhika Ghai. Eventually, we would fall in love and marry.

PARTIES AND PLACEMENTS

It was December 1994. New Year's Eve was round the corner as was my birthday, on 29 December. I decided to throw a big party at a nearby hotel. I hired a DJ to play the music and organized the liquor too.

On the night of the party the hotel was full of boys and girls. Then, to my surprise, some boys I had not invited turned up at the door. They had come not to join the party, but to beat me up for not inviting them! Their ringleader was someone named Laxmi Narayan, who was from a village in Uttar Pradesh.

While I somehow managed to avoid an ugly brawl with Laxmi and his boys, I learnt that I was not really universally popular as I had imagined. Many thought I was snooty and proud. Suddenly, it was like being that kid left out of the neighbourhood cliques all over again. But this time I was older and wiser. I was no longer weak and insecure. I had the support of 17 people who had joined the course from my management coaching centre. Most importantly, my confidence of being able to survive was also due to the fact that I was doing well academically, and—to my own surprise—I was quite a favourite with the ladies.

As the new year came around, I put the party incident behind me and concentrated on getting a good internship. I succeeded in getting one of the best internship offers from the equity firm Kotak Securities, which was a Kotak Mahindra and Goldman Sachs joint venture.

I also started dating Radhika and we spent a lot of time with each other.

The final semester was just three months away when I had to move out of the flat. The friend who was staying with me had also started dating by then, but things did not work out too well with him and his girlfriend and Radhika and I. Instead of telling him to move, I looked for a place nearby and shifted out.

By then the placement season was round the corner. I accompanied the faculty members to receive the companies that were visiting the campus. Kotak Securities, with whom I had interned, offered me a full-time job after my masters.

But back home things had taken a new turn. After thirty years of being employed, my father had quit his job and had decided to start his own construction company called Pinnacle Construction & Engineers in Chandigarh. I am happy to add that the name was suggested by me.

SPOILT FOR CHOICE

My father landed a big project to build the headquarters for a large corporation in Chandigarh. He made a lot of money from that project, and I, too, got some exposure to business by being around him and helping out.

I was still finishing my MBA when he started his business and from time to time I would go down from Indore and spend time with him.

I played a large role in the initial years of the company—from designing the logo to making the challan books. My father had been an engineer for four decades and lacked an understanding of the management control side—something that I had freshly learnt.

Suddenly I had too many choices—the Kotak offer was still on the table. Then there was my father's Pinnacle Construction & Engineers where I could join any time. Raman had expanded his business and had become a rich man, and had offered me a job at his firm.

However, Raman knew that I didn't like chartered accountancy much, so he gave me an offer I couldn't refuse. 'Why don't we get an approval from the Securities and Exchange Board of India (SEBI) to set up a merchant banking company, and you can run it,' he said. He had a client who was going public and there was plenty of work to do related to that. He suggested I join him. It wasn't a bad idea.

4

A PROMISE FULFILLED

When I was a boy, I remember my mother had once told us: '*Mera naam Savitri hai, lekin mujhe koi mere is naam se nahi bulata hai* (my name is Savitri, but no one calls me by this name).'

Somehow those words stuck in my mind. I had told her then that one day when we would start a company, it would be named after her. So I named my company Savitri Financial Services Limited.

This was 1996 and I was just 24 years old. I started working on my first client Venus Remedies. Even now it is a publicly listed company trading on the Bombay Stock Exchange (BSE).

With the liberalization that had been initiated in the early 1990s, India was changing. More international companies were coming to India to set up offices and we were becoming the destination for low-cost technology jobs.

One day I met Kumar Aulakh, the India head of the Denver-based company Quark Software. He was visiting my brother with another client of his, named Bal Sehgal, who owned a mineral water company. Bal wanted to take his company Nectar India public and had engaged our firm for the job. In those years Quark was bigger than Adobe, and was into the business of desktop publishing. They wanted to set up a development centre in India.

My brother asked me to make a presentation to Quark on why they should make Chandigarh their base.

Aulakh was convinced, but that was only half the job done. I then met the principal secretary of Punjab, Ramesh Inder Singh, and explained to him why Quark setting up a centre in Chandigarh was important, and how it would create a lot of jobs.

But to set up a centre Quark needed land on subsidy, 500 phone lines and very high bandwidth so that they could develop software and send it to the headquarters.

I made yet another presentation to the secretary. In those days large consulting firms like Boston Consulting Group (BCG) and McKinsey hardly did business in India. But I remember, before my meeting with the secretary, a bunch of consultants—who were there on some other business, all dressed sharply in suits and ties—had come to meet him. That left me a little underconfident. But self-doubt has always helped me. It pushes me to do better by making me dig within myself for reserves of courage and confidence.

My presentation went well and I managed to convince Ramesh Inder Singh Gill.

Getting a phone line was not so simple in those days. Sometimes it took months to get one connection. It had taken us two years to get a phone line for our residence and here we needed 500 of them. This was as difficult as setting up an appointment with the chief minister of the state.

Somehow I got all the work done. Kumar Aulakh was so impressed that he made me the founding director of the local entity of Quark.

Over the next few years, companies including Infosys, Dell, Airtel and many others set up offices in Chandigarh. Few know that Quark paved the way for these establishments.

Among the other things I dabbled in during that phase was promoting renewable energy. Those were also the days when shortage of electricity was one of the biggest concerns for the government. India had 100,000 MW of total installed capacity whereas it needed 250,000 MW. There were naphtha-based and oil-based traditional power plants and then there were small five- to ten-megawatt renewable energy plants, which used rice husk, wheat husk or municipal waste to produce electricity.

Renewable energy was a new thing and the technology was not 100 per cent proven. I started working with Haryana Renewable Energy Development Authority and Punjab Renewable Energy Development Authority to conduct viability checks. These organizations were well funded by the Asian Development Bank and the World Bank.

I was not a management consultant, but I had the capability to extrapolate and see things beyond the obvious and give a logical sense to them. So I created a forty-page report on how the husk would be collected, how it would be stored, how it would be burnt, what would be the cost and how much electricity it would produce.

My work involved a lot of travelling, and soon I found myself looking at tourism investments in Nepal. Birendra Bir Bikram Shah, the king of Nepal, awarded me in 1996 for my work in bringing investments into Nepal.

DELHI-INDORE-MUMBAI

By now I had dated Radhika for more than a year. Being a year junior to me in college she was still in Indore, finishing her masters.

I had to go to Mumbai quite often for meetings at the Reserve Bank of India (RBI) for the merchant banking business. For this, I would always take a flight from Chandigarh to Indore and then to Mumbai.

My brother didn't like this much and thought that I was wasting money and getting way too distracted. But I was madly in love.

I was also paying phone bills of Rs 30,000 a month then, and a large amount of this was because of my long conversations with Radhika. If I take inflation into account, that amount would be equivalent to Rs 1,12,000 today. My mother would get the shock of her life on seeing the bill, and I started hiding them from her.

The best option to reduce my expenses was to get married, and we did, on 16 June 1996. We were madly in love with each other. She was a little more than 22 and I was about to be 25.

A NEW BEGINNING

Around this time, I started working with the World Bank and the Asian Development Bank on some projects. It was my first real exposure to the US economy. I met a lot of travelling executives and the way they talked, their body language, the way they operated, everything fascinated me.

After my marriage, the family dynamics changed. Radhika was a modern girl, well qualified, with lots of friends and a great sense of fashion. I realized she was unable to show her true potential in our family setup. Yet our family had deep value systems and it would be unfortunate if I left the house and started staying separately. I was the youngest sibling, and everyone treated me like his or her child. That I had grown up and could handle the world on my own was something they could never understand.

Within a few months of my marriage the atmosphere at the house was making me unhappy. I was getting the same feeling that I got when I was working with my brother in his chartered accountancy firm—a feeling of emptiness.

None of this was hidden from my mother and one day she asked me straight out as to what was bothering me. 'You look sad, again,' she said. I told her the truth—about what was going on at home, and that was not just it; there was something more.

I was fascinated by international companies. I told her I wanted to work with an international company, not in India, but abroad.

My mother said that she would speak to Raman about it. Raman, as usual, had a solution. He suggested that I go to Singapore and find a job. A maternal uncle's daughter, my cousin, lived there with her husband and could help us find our feet. So Radhika and I decided to go to Singapore for five weeks.

SLEEPLESS IN SINGAPORE

The time in Singapore was not at all a honeymoon or a getaway. Every day, for almost seventeen to eighteen hours, I would search for jobs and apply for them. In those days email was not so common and accessing people was not easy. I would have to go to the market and buy something called a resume paper. Then, using my cousin's printer I would print my resume on those sheets. Then I would either post or deliver them personally to each of the offices.

For this, I bought a thick, 500-page financial directory, like the yellow pages. I searched for each and every bank, from the smallest to the biggest, and applied to them. On some days, I even printed up to a hundred resumes.

Some banks called me for an interview. But most of them politely rejected by thanking me for showing an interest in their company. The line they used was, 'We will keep your resume in our file and let you know when an opportunity matches your profile'.

I started getting a sinking feeling, not unlike my days at St Xavier's College, Mumbai, where I had gone for my MBA tutorials. The culture and people of Singapore overwhelmed me. My years of working as a merchant banker were not enough here and I could not turn around the interviews because my English wasn't very good. But I didn't give up. I kept applying.

Meanwhile, I remember Radhika and I celebrated our first Karva Chauth in Singapore. She was a constant support when every bank was rejecting me. She helped me prepare for interviews. But even that was of little help. I had gone into my shell by then—I was nervous and I couldn't talk much during those meetings.

I kept waiting for the right opportunity, which never came. Those five weeks were a period of extreme emotional struggle. My cousin still tells me that I worked like a machine in those weeks. Finally, I came back to India empty-handed and with a similar feeling I had when I had come back from Bikaner after failing in the MBA entrance interview.

BACK TO BASICS

Once we returned to Chandigarh, I helped Radhika start her own company, Abhivyakti Communications, an integrated advertising company. I spoke to one of my uncles to allow her to operate from his office, and he did.

At my own work front, I took up many more new assignments to keep myself busy and not think about my failure in Singapore. But none of this was giving me the happiness I wanted. I still wanted to work with a multinational.

I kept trying new things to divert myself. That was the time when Internet had come to Chandigarh. Offices and some homes were taking Internet connections. I decided to become an Internet service provider. I made a complete project report and did a viability study to estimate the cost of setting up the business.

But the trip to Singapore had opened my mind. I was very fascinated by how developed economies functioned and I realized that the only thing that would make me happy was to go abroad.

I decided to get back to studies once again and wrote the GMAT exams. It was already late, and the last date to apply to many universities had passed. I applied to the ones that were still taking in applications.

Once that was done, Radhika and I went to Dalhousie for our second anniversary. One day, when we were there, my mother called me. 'There is a letter for you from Washington University in St Louis,' she said.

The very next moment I ran to the nearby cyber cafe to check my email. I had received an email from the university asking me to send a photograph and a few other details. It did not say anything about my having got admission. I was happy that Washington University had responded but I wanted to be doubly sure before celebrating.

When I went back to Chandigarh, the first thing I did was read the letter. It said, 'Congratulations, you have been admitted to Washington University in the MBA program.'

This was sometime in June 1999. I sent them my acceptance note and deposited my admission fees. On 13 August 1999, Radhika and I took an Air France flight via Charles de Gaul airport in Paris to the US.

5

NOT BORN IN THE US

Radhika was better prepared for life in the US than I was. Unlike me, she spoke fluent English. And she had had more exposure to American culture and ideas. She also had friends in the US. She had grown up listening to rock and pop music—all that was alien to me, and she knew things like which cities were on the West Coast and which were on the East Coast. The more she talked about America, about New York, Chicago and other cities—most of which I would tour in my more-than-a-decade stay in the country—the more excited and nervous I got.

Before coming to the US, I had got in touch with the college and had given them details of my arrival. I was told that someone would be at the airport to receive me. But when we landed, we found to our dismay that no one had come to get us from St Louis airport.

Radhika used a pay phone to call one of her friends, Smriti Uppal, who was married and settled in the US. Those days very few could afford mobile phones, and fewer would use them for international calls. I was definitely not one of those who had a mobile phone then.

Smriti came with her husband Vikas to pick us up from the airport. We didn't have a place to stay so they took us to their home, where we spent the next few days. It was embarrassing to take their help right after landing. Theirs was a small apartment, and we had seven suitcases—all set to stay in the US for at least two years. In the back of our minds, however, was a bigger plan—something more permanent: to settle down in the US, get a high-paying job, have kids, see them grow up, and perhaps eventually shift to a quieter place just outside the city, and grow old together.

But destiny had different plans for me. I will come to that in the subsequent chapters.

TICKET TO RIDE

My university was 15 miles away from Smriti's house. It was impossible to take a cab to the university every day. I had very little money and even public transport would have been too expensive.

Every day Vikas would drop me to the university and on his way back from work, pick me up.

Our university had an Indian Club which looked into the welfare of Indian students at Washington University. It helped them settle in by assisting them in finding a house, arranging for flatmates, etc. The Club connected us to Anil Kaul, a Kashmiri pandit. Kaul was a simple, studious boy. He took good care of us, fed us and kept us warm till we found our own place. His house was closer to the university than Vikas's, and I could avail the shuttle service.

It took us almost a month to finalise an apartment. The one we chose was almost three miles away from the university, whereas Anil's house had been only half a mile from the university. But Radhika and I couldn't find something in our budget nearer to the college.

OUR FIRST HOUSE

For the first time, after four-and-a-half years of being married, we now had our own house, even though it was on rent. It was fascinating. Radhika spent a lot of time setting up the house. We bought some items for the kitchen, a few second-hand furniture items, and we were set.

Back in Chandigarh I used to drive a Maruti Esteem, which I had sold off before our move to the US. I used the money to buy a red, two-door, 1985 Toyota Tercel. Of the twelve Indian students who had joined the MBA programme that year, I was the first to buy a car.

After paying my college fees we were left with $1,000 a month. This would include the house rent, utility bills, telephone, petrol and so on. Most of the money came from my savings during my merchant banking days, and I took some help from my parents too.

Once we had moved in and settled down, Radhika would sometimes worry about her career and say that she wasn't doing anything. I told her to start studying again like I was doing. But the sessions had already started, so Radhika could join the university only a year later.

INTERNET AMERICA

While I was happily settling into a new country, America was going through a massive change. The reach of the Internet was growing wider and deeper. Little did I know then that the Internet would eventually become my bread and butter.

This was before the dotcom bubble burst and Internet companies were mushrooming by the dozen everyday. Many of them had already got listed.

In 1998, Amazon, which started as an online bookseller four years back, was becoming bigger with every passing day, and was the only stock that rose by 966 per cent in one year, wrote Floyd Norris in an article in *The New York Times.*[1]

The Internet was a funny thing. Not many understood the dynamics. Norris wrote, giving the example of Yahoo, one of the first Internet companies to get listed on the bourses:

> It more than doubled the day it went public—April 15, 1996—and within a few months had fallen back to the offering price. But an investor who put $1,000 into the stock at the close of trading that first day, and held on, would now have stock worth $80,500. That is more than ten times as much as someone who bought Microsoft

[1]Floyd Norris, 'The Year in the Markets; 1999: Extraordinary Winners and More Losers', *The New York Times*, 3 January 2000, Accessed on 11 March 2020, https://www.nytimes.com/2000/01/03/business/the-year-in-the-markets-1999-extraordinary-winners-and-more-losers.html.

the day it went public in 1986 would have had after the same amount of time.

Some didn't do as well. Value America, an e-tailer, which went public in April 1999 at $23 a share, and had gone up to $74.25 on the first day, ended the year at $5.06, after laying off many employees. Others like eToys traded at $26.25 by the end of the year, just above its offer price of $20. At its peak, the stock was trading at $86, in October 1999.

Norris wrote that the substantial gains of the Internet companies 'reflects the speculative fever gripping the market and is based on hopes that as the Internet transforms the economy, companies that did not exist a few years ago will become giants'.

Some of them did; Amazon has a market capitalization of $475 billion, and Google is worth $647 billion.

I had come to America when the country was going through the first dotcom boom. America Online (AOL) had acquired Time Warner for $160 bn; Yahoo's stock was going up $50 per day. The whole world wanted to be in America, and in America the place to be was in Silicon Valley. The Internet was compared to the 'industrial revolution', or the Gold Rush in Sacramento, or the Detroit automobile revolution.

Nowadays 98 per cent of American households have Internet connections—either through cable or wireless. Back in the day, less than half of America had access to the Internet.

In India, at the time, the Internet was still a luxury. Only offices used the Internet. For individuals, cyber cafes were where Internet was a medium to access quick porn or enter Yahoo! chatrooms to talk to strangers.

One of the first Internet lingos that became famous was 'ASL', which every boy and girl chatting on Yahoo would ask the person on the other side of the chat. ASL stood for 'age, sex, location' and was the starting line of many chats.

I never managed to be a part of that Internet journey, and I don't miss that either. I had no time to spend on these frivolous chatrooms, which were paving the way for the bigger Internet revolution.

UNITED NATIONS

By now my MBA programme had started, and once again I felt like a stranger amidst a large English-speaking crowd. The college assigned us to groups—later on students were allowed to make their own groups. These groups solved many problems—they brought people of various countries, ethnicities and origins close. They also helped in sharing study material. Some groups became so closely knit that they were like family to each other in this alien nation.

In our group there was Matt and Justin, both Americans, and Judy, who was from China. For the first time I was exposed to concepts like team building exercises, and that too with people from different nationalities. It was very different from the way we had studied MBA in Indore.

For me, if I ever stopped and thought, it was all quite remarkable. Here I was in the US, studying in a 150-year-old university; I had a house of my own, a small car, I was making new friends, and for the first time I was getting to know people from 45 different countries.

6

WINTER, BOLLYWOOD STYLE

Soon after our coursework began, we were told that we had to prepare for our internships during the summer break, between the first and second year of the MBA programme.

I also realized that I had to do everything—from building my resume to finding a company to intern with—on my own.

The first step was to build a resume. I had done this before, many times, especially when I was applying for jobs in Singapore. So I thought it would be quite easy. I drafted my resume and submitted it to one of our seniors—each first year student was assigned a senior to review the resume. 'It is a very Indian resume,' the person said. 'But you have a very interesting background—you have done so many jobs before coming to the US.'

For the rest of the evening we sat together and worked on the resume. He changed it completely and made it more 'American'.

By now, winter had come. For any person coming from a tropical or temperate type of climate, the first winter in America when the temperature drops many degrees below zero can be tough. The schools are shut and many students go back to India for vacations.

Radhika and I decided to stay back.

A senior faculty member, Mahendra Gupta, who later became one of the first Indians to become the dean of the business school, liked me. He also knew that I was married.

One day he invited us to his home and said, 'Winter is here, and you will not be able to step out of the house much. Take my television.' The television was an old model, but it worked fine and we were happy with it.

Mr Gupta had only one condition. He asked me to pass on the television to some other Indian student who would come to Washington and might need the company.

In those days there was no Netflix or Amazon Prime. So we bought a VCR. The VCR cost us $69. You might get a certified refurbished Amazon Echo speaker with artificial intelligence capabilities for the same amount today.

My next stop was the Indian store from where we bought some video cassettes of Bollywood movies and songs. Before that I had never thought that one day I would listen to Bollywood songs just to make myself feel close to home. I started remembering the times when while growing up, India's sole TV channel Doordarshan used to play songs from Bollywood movies and was very popular until the 1990s, before the advent of cable TV.

The winter break was also a good time to introspect. I had too many thoughts running through my mind and was scared that if I didn't get an internship or a job, I would go back home as a failure. Radhika's brother, who was also pursuing his MBA in the US, visited us. But I didn't let any of this distract me.

I started circulating my resume with all the financial services companies. Every night I would send a dozen emails to these companies, and the next day I would go to the college and call these companies up from there. The college had installed 50 telephones so that students could follow up on their job applications. When I visited the college to make those calls, I would often bump into Indian students—we were the ones who did not have money to go back home.

There were 200 students in the first year of the MBA programme and I was the first one to start looking for an internship. Soon winter was over, and summer was on its way. I had not yet secured an internship. There were twelve Indian students including me and the other eleven had got their internships. I was among the last 10 per cent students who had not got an internship.

THE AMERICAN DREAM

It hurt me even more because I was the only Indian in my college who had already visited Silicon Valley—home of the world's largest technology companies. The only two industries where I wanted to do my internship were financial services or technology startups.

In December 1999, I came to know that a career fair was about to happen in Silicon Valley. Radhika and I packed my bags and decided to spend the next three to four days in Silicon Valley, at the career fair.

The original price of the flight tickets was $600, and I couldn't afford that amount, so I bought the tickets through reverse auction on Priceline. My initial bid was $180, and I finally got the tickets for $200, but with two stopovers, which I didn't mind.

Like the rest of America, Silicon Valley was also new to us. We knew that Radhika's father's cousin, who was just a few years elder to me, was living there. But we were reluctant to take his help. But as luck would have it, when Radhika's mother came to know about our travel, she called Rahul Jairath, the cousin, to offer us some help. He gladly agreed.

Over the years Rahul and I have become close friends, but I was in complete awe of him when I met him for the first time. He had come to the airport to pick us up in his burgundy BMW 5 Series car. We hopped into his car—my first time in a BMW.

I still remember the song that was playing: 'I Will Survive' by Gloria Gainer. The song had an uncanny resemblance with what was happening in my life at that moment. I knew I would survive—survive the struggle of trying to find myself a toehold in America.

The car turned on to Highway 101. That's the road that connects San Francisco and Silicon Valley. Soon enough, I saw this huge board of Yahoo. All the companies I had only read about, and dreamt of working with, were all around me.

LIFE OF AN INTERN

It was 15 April. The summer break was just a month away. By now I had collected 37 rejection letters, which I still have in my possession.

They remind me of the tough days. Many agreed to meet me and interview me, many investment banking firms flew me to New York, Chicago, etc., but none gave me a job.

I often asked myself where I was going wrong. Internally, I was breaking down, but I could not let that show. I never told Radhika about my inner fears.

Then, on 16 April I got my first internship offer. As if the jinx was broken, between 16 April and 15 May, I got six internship offers. One of them even offered me double its initial offer.

Instead of one internship I picked up two offers. Most of my classmates did one 7–10 month internship and took a break. But I had big dreams, one of which was to get Radhika enrolled into the MBA programme, and it was expensive.

My first internship was with Charles Schwab, an investment banking firm headquartered in San Francisco, and the other with an Internet startup, Activa, funded by Sabeer Bhatia.

Bhatia was one of the most successful Internet entrepreneurs of Indian origin. He was the co-founder of Hotmail, one of the first email services, which was acquired by Microsoft in 1998 for a whopping $400 million.

7

DINNER WITH SABEER

Summer break started and I was off to San Francisco for three months for my internship with Charles Schwab. It would have been too expensive to stay in a hotel, so for the first few days we hired a motel, and stayed there until Radhika found a nice house near University of California, Berkeley.

By now Radhika had given her entrance exams and had also gotten through. It was time to celebrate—everything was going as per plan. She wanted to shop—from handbags to shoes to dresses. We also visited Disneyland for the first time. At Disneyland we bought a blue whale stuffed toy. We kept that in our car's boot and decided to courier the rest of the luggage home. But we did not take insurance for the baggage and the suitcases never reached my home. The police, too, said that they couldn't do much and all the clothes and other things that Radhika had bought with our hard-earned money were lost. We never got back any of it.

One evening, Sabeer Bhatia asked me to join him for dinner. So Naveen Singha from Activa and I headed out for dinner. It was fascinating meeting him. The guy who was a hero in my eyes was going to be sitting in front of me.

We met Sabeer somewhere midway. He took us in one of his luxury cars to an eating place where he spent about $300 over dinner. That was a lot of money considering that I had never spent more than $10–20 for dinner. I was very surprised, and nervous.

Sabeer had style; when he got off the car, he threw the car keys towards the valet and walked in nonchalantly.

Next, he invited us to a party in Tiburon. It is one of the small islands after the Golden Gate. Radhika and I bought new clothes for this party. At Tiburon he had a beautiful house with a big swimming pool, something I had never seen before.

From those two internships I earned $13,000. Soon after the internships, both the companies made me job offers. I decided to go with Charles Schwab as I had always wanted to work with a large investment banking company. In hindsight, I know I took the right decision—the dotcom bubble wiped off more than 70 per cent of the Internet businesses in America.

AMERICA IN PERIL

Businesses may fail, but entrepreneurs never fail—this is what I learnt from Sabeer Bhatia. He was one of the first entrepreneurs who made a lot of money and exited at the right time.

In the late 1990s, Internet service providers would provide email services, but they had their limitations. Emails could not be accessed from anywhere—they were tied down to the location of home or office, where the provider's service was available. With all the technology power and deep pockets, even the biggies—Microsoft, IBM and Cisco—had not managed to crack the way to make this happen.

Sabeer changed the way people used emails.

He had worked as a hardware engineer with Apple and later with Firepower Systems. At Apple he met Jack Smith, and later the duo built Hotmail, which they launched on 4 July 1996 on US's Independence Day. Hotmail allowed users to access emails from anywhere in the world on Internet provided by any service provider. It was Sabeer's 'aha' moment.

But that was it. Sabeer hasn't been quite successful with his other ventures since. He launched Arzoo, an e-commerce company, in 1999. He also launched JaxtrSMS, and said that JaxtrSMS would change the way people messaged, like Hotmail changed the way people sent emails. Arzoo and JaxtrSMS never achieved the kind of success that Hotmail did. The business of emails remains his favourite, and he has invested in email collaboration software, ccZen.

It was a privilege to work in a company he was associated with. But I chose to continue at another company, Charles Schwab, where I wanted to learn how the investment banking industry functioned.

I wanted to be a financial analyst at Wall Street, the mecca of the financial world.

Most people who went to the US at that time were either working for Microsoft, Cisco, Oracle or one of the other technology companies. In the twenty-first century, the US was the country you went to in order to fulfil your dreams, and I was no different.

Yet I did not want to be a technologist or a software engineer, so I chose to study MBA. I also thought that studying in the US was the best way to learn its culture. America was the country where I saw myself in future.

I started my summer internship at Charles Schwab.

THE JOB

Charles 'Chuck' Schwab was one of the fifty richest people in the world. He had founded Charles Schwab Corporation—a bank and brokerage house—in 1971.

What was interesting is that only seven years ago, in 1963, Charles and two more people started *Investment Indicators*, an investment advisory newsletter. At its peak, in 1963, there were 3,000 people who paid $84 a year to subscribe to their newsletter. In April of 1971, the firm was incorporated in California as First Commander Corporation, a fully owned subsidiary of Commander Industries, Inc. A year later, Charles bought all the stock of the company and renamed it Charles Schwab & Co., Inc.

I had never worked with someone like Charles. I would often observe him from a distance, whenever he would be in the office. He was a man of great composure and hardly ever got flustered or angry. He believed success came from understanding and executing the details. Little did I know that my observations of Charles would help me build two successful e-commerce companies more than a decade later.

When ShopClues was being built it was important to look into the minutest things—from the technology to how the pictures were looking when they were being uploaded to whether the courier partners were delivering on time. Also, being the first true marketplace, there was no precedence to the business, and many of the things we did, like getting local merchants to sell on our platform, were happening for the first time in India's e-commerce business.

As a management intern I was determined to make a mark in the Management Associate Program. I was the only one from my business school to be accepted in the programme—everyone else was from Yale, Harvard or Wharton, or from the other top business school in the US. That made me nervous as well as confident at the same time. Nervous because I thought that my competition had better exposure, and confident because had I not been as good as them I wouldn't have been a part of the programme. I worked tirelessly to make my presence felt. By the end, I was rewarded with a job offer from Charles Schwab even before the placement season had started.

That was ironical—I had been one of the last to get an internship but one of the first to get a job in a class of 200 students. While most of my classmates struggled to keep up their scores and worried about their jobs, I enjoyed my second year in college. Radhika, too, had started attending college now.

I had made some money from my internships at Charles Schwab and Activa and every evening there was something new—a new restaurant, a new bar, a movie or friends coming over for dinner at home. I had diligently checked out almost all the bars in town.

8

THE BIG BUST

Late 2000 was the beginning of the fading of the dream for many young entrepreneurs. Dotcom companies or Internet companies across the US were collapsing.

Three months after I had started my MBA, I remember AOL, which had bought Netscape in 1998, merged with Time Warner in a deal that was estimated to be $165 billion.

It was one of the biggest mergers in those days, but soon became the most spectacular failed merger and caused huge losses.

When the Internet economy started collapsing, every company faced problems. AOL collapsed. Yahoo collapsed. Many of my friends had job offers from these companies. The companies had been interviewing candidates between January and May. Suddenly, they started taking back job offers or delaying them.

It was a scary situation. The parties stopped and so did the club hopping. Every morning I would wake up in fear, and would head straight to the college and open my inbox to check if Charles Schwab has rescinded the offer.

I couldn't take a chance, so I started applying for interviews and jobs in other companies in case Charles Schwab took back its offer letter. They didn't.

Then it was time for Radhika to apply for an internship. She had got an offer from Goldman Sachs in New York. I decided to take a break and stay with her in New York for the next one and a half months. But something surprising happened in the last two weeks of her internship—Goldman sent Radhika to Silicon Valley.

Here we stayed in Sheraton, just outside Stanford University. After two weeks Radhika returned to her college in St Louis and I stayed back for my job at Charles Schwab. I had about a month to set up things and move into a flat before joining Charles Schwab on 6 September.

Amit Khetan, a friend from St Louis, and I moved into an apartment. For nearly one year I would have to stay without Radhika, till the time she finished her MBA. Amit had joined Cisco, which was in the vicinity.

This time I was setting up everything without my wife. That wasn't such a good feeling. Every week I would go and buy things for the house—some chairs, a table and kitchenware. Apart from Amit, I had a few more friends from Activa, with whom I spent my evenings.

DIALLING 911 ON 9/11

I had managed to get a couple of other job offers, but none of them was as good as Charles Schwab. Though I was setting up home in Silicon Valley, I was not sure about my status. Every day I would get to know of friends either losing their jobs or being told to defer their joining dates. Newspapers were full of gloom and doom. It was quite depressing.

But even in the first week of September there was no mail from Charles Schwab, and so, finally, on 6 September 2001, I joined them.

Charles himself welcomed the Management Associate Program joiners—I was one of them. His speech was short and sweet. I still remember his words: 'This is a leadership programme,' he told all of us. We were given a bag and a t-shirt each.

It wasn't that Charles Schwab wasn't going through a tough time. The dotcom bust had impacted all companies—big and small, and in all businesses. When I had joined Charles Schwab it had a large 26,000-employee base. When I left it had almost halved to 14,000 employees.

Five days after I joined Charles Schwab, early in the morning Amit and I started getting calls from our parents. Both of us missed the calls the first and second times. By the time we picked up, they were frantic.

'Are you fine? What's happening in the US?' my mother asked me.

I had no clue what she was talking about. Everything was fine when I had gone to sleep the previous night.

'It's showing on TV that terrorists have blown up some buildings,' she said.

We didn't have a television till then, so Amit and I quickly went to the nearest store that sold televisions and bought one.

The 9/11 (11 September 2001) attacks were the worst in America's history. Al-Qaeda had hijacked four passenger aircrafts to orchestrate four attacks that had killed nearly 3,000 people.

Two planes crashed into the north and south towers of the World Trade Centre (WTC) in New York, resulting in the collapse of the 110-storey buildings. A third plane crashed into the Pentagon, headquarters of the United States' Department of Defence. A fourth plane crashed into a field in Stonycreek township near Shanks Ville, Pennsylvania.

That was the last nail in the already failing economy of America caused by the dotcom bust. Now the economy completely collapsed. There were job losses all over, but Charles Schwab stood by us—every single management programme trainee it hired.

FINDING MY FEET AGAIN

I completed my first month of training, and then they put us on three rotations of six months each in different departments so they could absorb us.

In one of the rotations I worked directly with the senior vice president of the company. That was quite unusual as I was just a trainee. It was in the mutual funds department—one that by no stretch of imagination was a small tucked-away-into-the-corner business unit. It was a $190 billion mutual fund.

They liked my analytical skills and I got my first task. 'Can you build a financial model which will rate 5,000 different banks based on credit score between one and five, five being the best and one being the worst?'

With that brief I started working on the project. The mutual funds were invested in various banks and money market funds, and Charles Schwab wanted to do a credit risk analysis of these funds. I worked in this department for the next six months.

I started feeling like I had in Mumbai where I had gone to prepare for my MBA entrance test examination in 1993—I was amidst a lot of people who were culturally different. Every single person in the team was an American, all from business schools better than mine. But this time it was different. My colleagues were very supportive—they said they liked my energy and willingness to experiment. I always had a lot of academic curiosity and that contagious energy led others to collaborate with me.

A senior (I can't remember his name now) taught me advanced Excel sheet usage to make financial modelling. Finally I built the financial model. The chief investment officer of that department never talked to or met any newcomer. He called me in and sat down with my presentation. He was quite impressed with what I had done.

This made me think that finally I was in a department that would absorb me. I had given my best. But every department was conscious of the head count and none of them wanted to make even a single addition to the existing team. Things were getting difficult. How long would I keep floating from department to department without a proper seat?

By then employees of Charles Schwab had started losing their jobs. I still had mine.

Soon I was paired with another senior vice president to implement something that is called the 'value at risk' (VAR). Value at risk had come into being after a famous failure. A hedge fund called Long-Term Capital Management (LTCM) started by two Nobel prize winners basically created the fund, which was going to make a lot of money based on some algorithm.

According to this algorithm, once in 500 million times they would lose a lot of money. But they did not know when that would happen. It was unfortunate that it happened in the first year of starting the business.

That led to the concept that any financial institution with one billion or more of public money in the stock market must calculate every day how much money is at risk based on the market volatility. Charles Schwab had more than a billion of public money and they were required by the Federal Bank of America to implement 'value at risk'.

The senior vice president and I, between us, implemented the VAR for the entire company. I learnt a lot. She was a tough manager and I had a difficult time working with her. Charles Schwab also had a stockbroker unit, and I was pulled in there for the job of finding out how much it cost the company to execute one order. For example, if someone purchased a hundred shares of ACC Cement, what would be the cost incurred to buy and maintain that stock? The company wanted to implement something called Activity Based Costing (ABC). A professor at Harvard University had developed the concept.

It wasn't very difficult for me to do that. But the only problem was that it was a little boring. It reminded me of my chartered accountancy days in Chandigarh. The good part was that Charles Schwab made use of a lot of technology tools, and my thirst to learn more was driving me. Add to that the fact that I was afraid of losing the only job I had. I had an educational loan to pay off, worth $250,000. That burden would bother me constantly.

Going back to India was not an option, so while an average American worked for seven to eight hours, I spent twelve to fourteen hours in the office and then worked at home.

Though I did not like accounting much, I did a very good job of implementing ABC. That allowed me to learn a lot of new things. This department interacted closely with the technology department since much of the costing from the stock business was done with the use of technology.

By now I had two successful implementations under my name. The managers of the accounting division felt pressurized by the human resource team to absorb me. I kept my fingers crossed. But times were bad and there was a mandate from the headquarters to reduce cost, not to add to it. No one had an open head count; everyone had a mandate to shrink. Still I stayed with this department for the next six months. Salaries were coming on time, thankfully.

My job description and my achievements were floated within the other departments of Charles Schwab. Since I had worked very closely with the technology department, they knew what I could do. Finally the technology department absorbed me as a senior financial consultant, a role that was equivalent to senior manager of finance.

9

THE WORLD BEFORE AMAZON

My work at Charles Schwab helped me, and the downturn threw up new opportunities. Suddenly the market of strategy planning opened up. My role was to do costing for various technology infrastructures.

One day I was called into a meeting where the top-level team of the business unit was sitting. It was a daylong huddle on how to reduce technology cost. When I was summoned, I panicked thinking I was getting called in to be fired. Already many people had been asked to quit their jobs.

I was in for a surprise. One of the main jobs was handed over to me—that of reducing technology cost by $200 million. It was a high-profile assignment and I worked with the finance head of the department and some of the seniormost technology people in the next couple of months.

In those days Charles Schwab was considered to be one of the top technology companies. Google's first chief technology officer Brad Goldberg was working in the same department. We sat together in the same bay. He left Charles Schwab to join Google that was just coming up and few knew about it. Fewer trusted in Internet companies any longer after the dotcom bust. Most people thought that Brad had made a bad move. 'He is joining a startup company,' they whispered.

Brad and I worked together on the project. It was a new learning curve for me. I learnt about data centres, server cost and cost of implementing PCs, among other technology costs. The concept of cloud computing hardly existed. All the data of a company was stored in large servers owned by Charles Schwab, unlike now, when one can store data by paying rent to Amazon, Microsoft and Google. There is a lot of flexibility now—one can increase and decrease the space as per the company's requirement and pricing is done accordingly. But this was the pre-cloud-computing era. I studied what was happening in the world of technology and what new innovations technology companies were coming up with. My summer internship with Activa helped me. For Internet companies, everything was supposed to be on the web, not on-premise. Although it was one and a half years since my internship with Activa, it had helped me develop deep knowledge about technology, application development and IT infrastructure.

Amazon Web Services was yet to appear and some companies

like HP, Hitachi and IBM offered customized computing-on-demand solutions.

I suggested something that would change Charles Schwab's IT infrastructure forever. It was to reduce the capacity of Charles Schwab's own computing power and outsource the excess capacity to computing-on-demand. That way we could use minimum infrastructure, and rely on external space and computing. Having everything in-house meant we had to deploy infrastructure keeping in mind peak capacity, and were incurring the cost of the peak infrastructure throughout the year.

I made the recommendation of reducing the infrastructure by 40 per cent. For a financial company it was a tough call to take. They were afraid of data leak—something that still bothers banks and financial services companies in India and the world over. After a lot of deliberation Charles Schwab implemented it, and the company, for the first time since its inception, moved to what is now called a 'hybrid model', where a percentage of IT infrastructure is owned by companies, and the rest is outsourced.

ON WIFE'S TRAIL

It was mid-2002 when Radhika finished her graduation. The American economy was slowly recovering and fewer people were losing their jobs, but new jobs were still a rarity.

Radhika went from pillar to post, but she was unable to get a job. Even my job wasn't secure. People who retained their jobs felt blessed. It was one of the biggest crises I faced in America.

To add to my insecurities, none of the people who had been involved in my hiring were there in the company any longer—some of them had lost their jobs and others had left for more stable options. For the first two and a half years I lived in a lot of fear, and for all the right reasons. It was not about just losing a job, it was about losing the right to live in the US.

Finally Radhika found a job. It was an entry-level unimpressive job, in Seattle, where one of our MBA school alumni was a senior person and hired Radhika. But it was important for her to take up that job.

We decided that Radhika would move to Seattle, and every weekend either I would travel to Seattle or she would come down to San Francisco.

My fear of losing my job was so high that I had even thought that in case I lost my job, I would shift to Seattle with Radhika and look for work there.

Radhika had barely settled in when she called me one morning and said that she was pregnant. I was ecstatic at the thought of becoming a father but worried, too, due to the uncertainties on the job front.

Making matters worse, Radhika was having a troubled pregnancy, and she decided to come back to San Francisco. Companies in the US offer long-term disability leave during pregnancy, which Radhika availed. That allowed her to be away from work for a year, without any pay cut.

In November 2003, our son Ahaan was born. Radhika's long-term disability was coming to an end and she was unsure about re-joining her office. It was a choice between company loyalty and work ethics, and motherhood.

The company got in touch with Radhika, and told her that it would be great if she could join back. Radhika, meanwhile, was thinking about looking for a job in San Francisco. She applied to many offices, but she didn't find one. She had only one year of experience in Seattle, and almost negligible experience back in India.

In Silicon Valley most of the jobs were technology jobs. Also, in those days, technology companies were only hiring techies. So, one day Radhika told me, 'Why don't you look for a job in Seattle?' If I did that, then she could continue where she was working.

In the first week of December 2003, I started applying in many places. I started with making a list of companies in Seattle—Microsoft, Costco, Amazon, Expedia and a couple of other companies. Microsoft was the best at that time. Amazon was small, Apple was nowhere in the picture and Google was not of the size it is today.

Luckily I got an offer from Microsoft. It wasn't an easy process. Everyday Microsoft used to get 3,000 applications. A day after I applied, I got a call from the recruiter. 'We liked your resume; can we set up a call sometime?' they asked.

I had no reason to refuse Microsoft. We spoke for an hour on the phone. The next I knew I was travelling to Seattle for multiple rounds of interviews at Microsoft.

Somehow I resonated well with Microsoft's culture: passionate, with a workforce of academically curious and collaborative people who were intellectually driven. This was around 15 December 2003. Till Christmas I didn't hear from them and I almost lost hope.

It wasn't a very happy New Year for me. The first week of January passed. Then, on 9 January 2004, I got a call. 'Sorry for the delay; are you still open for the job at Microsoft?' the recruiter asked.

I kept quiet for a minute—a strange feeling was welling up inside me. I knew that I had got the job, only that I couldn't have shouted out of excitement into the phone.

'Everyone you met here in Seattle is happy with you... We want to make you an offer,' the person on the other end said. But they didn't offer me a hike in my salary. They knew that Radhika lived and worked in Seattle, and they took advantage of my situation.

The logic they gave me was that in California you pay 9 per cent state tax and in Seattle there is no state tax, and that was my increase in salary. End of February, I resigned from Charles Schwab and Radhika and I moved to Seattle.

Microsoft gave us corporate housing. We had a four-month-old baby now. I bought a Nissan Pathfinder car, a 4×4. We also bought a BMW. A brand new BMW had been returned by the buyer because of a manufacturing defect, and that car came back to the market after refurbishment—a certified BMW at a BMW dealership. I could not afford a brand new BMW at that time, which cost roughly $38,000. I bought this one for $22,000.

For the first time I felt that life was great. For the first time we felt fully settled in America.

10

HELLO MR BILL GATES

Not long after I joined Microsoft, my boss walked up to me, looking worried and excited at the same time. He said, 'Be ready to meet Bill Gates and Steve Ballmer.'

For a moment I thought he was joking. Why would Gates, founder of Microsoft, and Ballmer, Microsoft's CEO, want to meet me? In those days Microsoft had 78,000 people on its payroll and another 50,000 on contractual jobs. Very few of them ever got a chance to meet Gates and Ballmer, and fewer got a chance to work with them.

My boss wasn't joking. Exactly two weeks after the conversation, he told me to prepare a presentation for Steve Ballmer. People who worked in Microsoft at that time told me, and it was obvious to me too, that this was a big opportunity for a fresher like me.

What was the presentation about? Microsoft and Intel used to work closely to build software and chips for computers. Intel's CEO Craig R. Barrett who was known for making the best and the most powerful microprocessors had a review meeting with Steve Ballmer. I had to prepare a presentation around Intel's long-standing relationship with Microsoft when they would have a set of new discussions on how Microsoft and Intel could collaborate better.

It was all about personal computers (PCs) then. The growth in use of personal computers was one of the parameters the Federal Reserve Bank used to predict the growth in gross domestic product (GDP) of the country.

Often executives from the Federal Bank would come and meet executives in Microsoft. It was fascinating to see that. There were other companies that the Federal Bank spoke to—Dell and HP—but the PC makers could give only their own sales numbers of various countries. Microsoft's software was installed in all PCs. Apart from research firms like Gartner and IDC, it was only Microsoft that had the consolidated numbers of PC sales. Except for software piracy and open source platforms like Linux, it was Microsoft everywhere. Every PC had to work with Microsoft. All this made my assignment even more meaningful.

In those days Microsoft sold millions of licences annually. India was a tenth of the annual requirement. But software piracy was also high in India—at about 60 to 65 per cent. The US had 25 per cent, Western Europe had 35 per cent, Latin America had close to

50 per cent, China had 85 per cent, but Japan had only one per cent software piracy.

Ballmer would use the presentation that I was preparing in his meetings. In the next few months to come, I would take this presentation and travel to 12–13 countries. Everything was so fascinating—for the first time I got to understand the true meaning of a multinational company. I wasn't in the Indian subsidiary of a multinational. I was at the headquarters, working right under the nose of Microsoft's leadership.

THAI CONNECTION

Alongside the presentation for Ballmer, I was working on 7–8 other assignments. One of them was to make a report on a new version of software. The Thailand government was launching a cheap personal computer for every student in the country and the schools would provide these.

Bill Gates had committed to Thailand's prime minister that Microsoft would be a partner and provide those PCs with the Windows operating system, though a stripped-down version, at a low price. He convinced them not to use an open source operating system.

I was part of the team that was working on that product. It was a version of the Windows Vista operating system, and I was doing the pricing analysis.

Things moved smoothly for me.

In 2005, as he had been for a decade, Bill Gates was going to give the keynote address at the Las Vegas consumer electronics show. A couple of months before the show that year, I was roped into the team that would make the presentation for the keynote that year.

It was an opportunity that one working at Microsoft could only dream of. All of a sudden I was a popular person. Microsoft offices around the world started inviting me as a speaker.

I remember once I was invited to Taiwan as a speaker, along with the Asia Pacific head of Dell, HP and Acer. I was to talk about trends in the PC market. The topic was just up my alley.

All of a sudden just before the talk I remembered how I had run away from Mumbai to Chandigarh because I couldn't speak English well. I also remembered how I couldn't clear interviews because I couldn't perform well in group discussions. And now here I was, standing in front of a huge crowd, ready to deliver a speech in English. I was smiling to myself. I had overcome one of my biggest fears. While Charles Schwab was a platform into the big professional world, Microsoft had made me more confident, fearless and wise.

In many ways joining Microsoft was the biggest pivot in my life.

COMPLACENCY—A THREAT TO LEADERSHIP

In 2002, when I moved to Seattle after taking up the job with Microsoft, I was a part of Microsoft's PC market team. My team's role was to provide Microsoft with market intelligence, and my job was to estimate the size of the PC market quarterly and annually. Later on, I focused on opportunities in the emerging markets, India being a part of it. Some of the other areas in which I worked were software piracy and why people do piracy. A lot of my work also involved analysing Microsoft's threat from open source.

Microsoft was a clear market leader for both Windows as well as its Office Suite, which included Word, Excel and PowerPoint, among others. Google was then emerging as a new technology company and people at Microsoft thought of it as a flash in the pan. In some ways, Google was what Uber was in 2013—a company that everyone was talking about, and one of the hottest technology companies, but no one was scared of it.

And then, in August 2004, Google filed for its Initial Public Offer (IPO). Suddenly people at Microsoft sat up and took notice. In the IPO it was valued at $23 billion. Microsoft had a market capitalization of around $290 billion.

Little did I know that years later Google would surpass Microsoft in market capitalization. From being a leader, Microsoft would become a close follower. It would try to crack the mobile operating market where Google had a lion's share with Android. It would build tools of artificial intelligence just like Google. It would create a voice assistant called Cortana to compete with Google's Assistant. But in all this Google would remain ahead.

Microsoft didn't care about Apple either. Apple had made some name with the iPod (the portable music storage and playing device), which was first launched in 2001. With the iPod, Apple had shown that even in a cluttered market there was always space to have a successful product, even at a high price. There were many MP3 players. Most of the devices were available between $20 and $40. The iPod was for $200. In those days Microsoft didn't allow its employees to use any outside product inside the office.

Apple had not launched the iPhone yet, which would completely change the way computing and communication is done, making lives difficult for those in Microsoft. But in those days Apple hardly had 2 per cent market share in the hardware segment. For the longest time it continued to stay at that 2 per cent market share.

After the iPhone was launched, and when the devices made it to the masses, Google, Facebook (FB) and many others changed from PC-first to mobile-first.

In the presentation I created for Steve Ballmer, I had mentioned Apple, but no one bothered about them. When the slide with Apple would pop up, it would be dismissed. Nobody even saw Google as a threat.

For them, the real threat was open source software. That was much more visible in the market. The world was still migrating towards open source from a system of proprietary technology.

In fact, many competitors were slowly and quietly building their enterprises. E-commerce had not grown, and in the Internet space the battle was about Internet advertising. Google was slowly making inroads in this area. Microsoft had its own digital advertising play through MSN. But MSN was not mainstream for Microsoft. They did not think that the Internet would one day be as big and important as it did become.

11

FAMILY COMES FIRST

We were now living the great American dream—in a land of opportunities, where every underdog gets a chance to perform and excel.

Radhika and I ended up buying our first house. It was a beautiful four-bedroom house by the side of a lake. We also had a decent circle of friends.

While Radhika and I were working, our son would be at the daycare. For some reason, he started keeping unwell. We figured his immunity needed to get stronger, or he would keep picking up some bug or the other at the daycare. This went on for almost two years before his immunity was strong enough.

Coincidentally, Radhika started having some minor issues at her workplace at this time. She had already gone through ups and downs during the pregnancy, and changing cities. Now it was becoming emotionally traumatic to see our son suffering most of the time. Often she told me that she wanted to spend more time with our son and perhaps give up working. Her words made me think that I should start looking for a job that would pay enough so that Radhika did not have to work, and had ample time to raise Ahaan. At the same time I did not want to compromise on our lifestyle.

I was well paid, but I thought I deserved more. And more than that, somewhere at the back of my mind I always felt bad that Microsoft had not given me a salary hike when I had joined the company. I met the people from Microsoft's human resource department. They said that in due course the salary would get corrected.

But I needed the money now.

IN SEARCH OF A NEW DESTINATION

In 2004, I reconnected with Raheel Siddique—a bright chap from Delhi, whom I had first met in 1999 while doing my MBA in St Louis. After completing his graduation from Indian Institute of Technology (IIT) Delhi, he had joined Columbia University to complete his MBA programme. He used to work with a company called Monsanto, which was the largest biotechnology firm in the world.

Then Raheel joined Lehman Brothers as a Wall Street analyst. One day, we were at a movie hall, where Rahul pointed out that the kind of work I was doing at Microsoft was actually very valuable on Wall Street.

It sounded like a good proposition. So I started scouting for jobs as an analyst with financial services firms.

The first one that called me for an interview was Deutsche Bank. I met them and the interview was fascinating—I was getting into the world of financial services once again. But perhaps luck wasn't on my side at this time. The position went on hold. I continued working with Microsoft. Yet, the desire to move was growing and one fine day I realized that I didn't want to be with Microsoft anymore.

The same day I applied in five or six investment banks like Bernstein and Lehman Brothers, among others.

This was the summer of 2005.

All of a sudden I started getting calls for interviews. I flew to New York several times for interviews, and many of them happened on calls too. I started getting multiple job offers. These were in research teams covering hardware and software companies.

One day Vik Mehta, a friend's brother-in-law, who later became a very close friend of mine, came over for lunch. We went to the Microsoft museum together and talked a lot about the current state of my life—how I wanted to get out of Microsoft and become an analyst.

Vik called me after a few days. 'Sandeep, I know this analyst Mark Mahaney. He works in Citi Group as a senior analyst covering Internet companies. In the past he has worked with Mary Meeker.'

I was not confident about covering Internet companies. 'I know hardware and software, Vik,' I told him.

'All that doesn't matter. I think you know Internet equally well,' he said.

I was in two minds, wondering if I should plunge into the Internet space. In all this I had forgotten that I had been involved with studying the Internet space since 1999 in my MBA programme. I had worked with a faculty member on a consulting assignment to help a traditional company use the Internet in an efficient manner to do better business. I had also written the first Internet marketing course with that professor as his research assistant. Later on, I had worked for Activa, an Internet-born company.

I decided to talk to Mahaney, and Vik introduced me to him.

One day, I was taking my son to the daycare in the morning. Radhika went to work as usual at 7.30. It was my job to drop my son to the daycare, and Radhika would pick him up at five in the evening on her way back home.

I got a call. 'Hello, it's Mark Mahaney. Can we talk on the phone?' he said.

'I am dropping my son to the daycare, so there might be some background noise, but we can talk,' I replied.

The conversation was almost like an interview—mostly to know about the things that I was working on at Microsoft.

He called me back exactly after one and a half hours, and asked if I could travel to San Francisco, where he had lined up a series of meetings with Citi Group's IT hardware analyst, IT software analyst, semiconductor analyst and himself.

The next day I got a call from Jonathan Rosenzweig, who was the head of research for Citi Group. 'Sandeep, Mark really likes you, and so do the others whom you met.'

I had two more offers, and one of them was from Bear Sterns. I was in touch with Vik throughout the process. He said that the Internet was the future, and I should go ahead with that in mind and if I went for an industry with higher growth potential, I would never regret it. So, finally I joined Mark Mahaney, and worked with him for the next couple of years.

12

RUNNING ON WALL STREET

The decision to leave Microsoft was extremely difficult. Apart from the amazing opportunities that had come my way while working in the largest technology company in the world, my bosses were great and I loved the work. Even on my last day there, I was told, 'In case your new gig doesn't work out, come back. Our doors are always open for you.' In those days, very few Indians were given that kind of respect in an American company. The reassurance of having a back-up job meant a lot to someone like me who was still finding his feet in the US. While I left with more than a tinge of sadness, my confidence in my abilities went up a few notches.

I moved to San Francisco and started working with Citi in September 2005. America's economy was getting back in shape. At that point, Radhika decided to quit her job to take care of our kids. Given how passionate Radhika was about her job, I know it was a huge sacrifice. Radhika had to work until December to complete the projects she was working on. For the next three months, I would go back to Seattle every weekend to be with my family. It was déjà vu. My father had done the same thing when I was young. He would visit us in Kalka on weekends and go back to Chandigarh on Mondays.

We wanted to sell the house in Seattle and settle in San Francisco. The process of finding a buyer, however, turned out to be fairly painful. We had to decorate the house every weekend to woo the buyers, and the routine went on for a few months. We could not sell the house and ended up keeping it, the house I continue to own for 16 years now.

LIFE IN A CUBICLE

New-age workspaces are all about informality and breaking down hierarchies. I follow this culture at Droom, and did the same when I started ShopClues. There are open offices, where people sit in close proximity, which helps them discuss ideas and collaborate better. At Droom, I sit in an open space.

However, financial services firms like Citi are different because of the nature of the business, where a high level of operational secrecy is needed. Life in a financial services company was very different from Microsoft. Everything was quite formal at Citi as well as hierarchical. The size of your cabin increased as you went higher up in the pecking order.

Given that my work was largely focused on market research, I had to reach office well before the stock market opened. I had to wake up at 3:30 a.m. to reach office by 4:30 in the morning. I was given a cabin and a large part of the day was spent on phone calls with clients or writing reports. I had always been very conscious of my English-speaking abilities and this new job made life very tough indeed. I took the challenge head-on and decided that the best way to overcome my shyness was to speak more and more. Yes, I would make mistakes, but that's the only way to learn and become more confident. If that wasn't enough, I had to write a lot of reports, which was not my strength. The added pressure of writing them quickly made the task even more daunting. The urgency was because the information emerging from Wall Street would get outdated very fast and time was of the essence. This trial by fire not only made me stronger but also helped me realize that I had the ability to push myself even more.

Matthew Reichek, who was part of the same team, had joined a month before I did. We had a couple of things in common. He was from Seattle, too, and had come from a technology company, Expedia. I was the second to join Mark Mahaney. Our job was to focus on companies related to the Internet space. While Matthew's domain was e-commerce companies, I was to monitor Internet advertising companies like Google, Yahoo, Facebook and LinkedIn, among others. I was perceived as a natural fit for the job and more so because of my knowledge of the working of Google's rival, Microsoft. I felt quite lucky because e-commerce wasn't such a big thing back then, at least in the US.

Waking up early, long hours and no exercise started taking a toll on my health. The weekend travels to Seattle made it even more difficult. But that's how it is in a research profession on Wall Street.

ALL ABOUT GOOGLE

A month after I joined Citi, it was the quarterly results season—one of the four high points of a financial analyst's life. All listed Internet companies were about to post their financial results for July–September. Google reported its quarterly numbers, followed by Yahoo, Expedia and the others. It was the first time I was involved in this frenzy. Our job was to predict the future of the company by analysing its current financial state as well as identifying the key components of its future growth. Sounds simple, right? Throw in the fact that we had to pore over hundreds of pages of data, look at many thousand charts and carefully consider the millions of permutations and combinations, and then unravel if there were any red flags buried inside the data. All this had to be done in less than 12 hours.

My assessment would then form the basis for individuals and institutions to invest in these companies. But like any analyst worth his salt, I had already spent days researching these companies beforehand, reading and watching every announcement they made, and news that came out on them. I also had the benefit of having an existing financial model of the company from the previous quarter, which I had to upgrade in order to accurately make my financial predictions.

Every quarter, just after the results were declared, the companies would hold 'earning calls'. On these calls, the senior management of the concerned company would take questions asked by analysts from various financial services firms. My first earning call was with Google. I was given the opportunity by Mark to interact with Larry Page and

Sergey Brin, Google's founders. It was not only the first time I was hearing their voice, but also the first time I realized that even the men who run the most powerful companies are accountable. The question–answers were mostly clarifications we needed for our report. 'How much are you budgeting for stock options? How much would Western Europe account for in the overall business?' Both of them answered each and every question diligently and cogently. The call with Google was followed by many more such calls with the heads of other companies.

These direct interactions helped us fill the gaps in our analysis, and that in turn formed the basis for our investors to decide whether to buy, retain or sell the stocks of a particular company. All this was fascinating and every single minute spent at Citi helped me gain insight and knowledge into how the best minds think and how the best companies plan their growth.

Mark was like a mentor to me. He taught me the art of articulating complicated questions crisply. He also taught me how to sift through data and come up with questions that are relevant to a company's future. This art was important because each analyst firm would get only five minutes with the company bosses during the earning calls. I would send Mark a list of questions before such calls. Being the senior analyst, it was predominantly Mark who asked the questions, but he also gave me the opportunity to pose some questions. After those five minutes, Mark would end with one last question to the company bosses, 'Is there anything that you think is important and I did not ask?' This way he ensured that the company also got the chance to put forward anything that might be important, including future plans, for analysts to know but not covered adequately in the report.

Within just one year at Citi, the All American's Equity Research Rankings rated our team—Mark, Matthew and me—as the number one research team in the world in the Internet companies' research domain. We had won the Oscar of the financial research world! While number-crunching and generating data had always been my strength and I had trained myself to speak English confidently, my grammar was terrible. Mark would review the reports I wrote to correct the grammar. We worked very well as a team—each of us pooling in our strengths and making up for the other person's weaknesses—in this case, mostly mine. End result: we created a kickass financial model for each of the companies we tracked. We knew their positives and negatives inside out.

What really worked in my favour was the earlier exposure to the world of Internet and technology. I also realized how right Vik Mehta had been in scouting this job for me. It was also a great opportunity for me to learn. After all, I was surrounded by some of the best research analysts in the business, each covering cutting-edge companies, from computer hardware, software and semiconductors to new-age energy firms and the Internet. While there were 35 researchers on my floor, I felt lucky because I knew I was focusing on the coolest and the most happening company in the world—Google.

VIK MEHTA—MY FRIEND, MY GUIDE

Vik had a huge influence on my career. Had it not been for him, I would not have entered the financial world. I met Vik because of Ambrish Srivastava and Ambrish because of Rahul Jairath. Even today, I know Vik is just a phone call away.

After business school in 2001, I had moved to San Francisco for my first job. There I met Rahul Jairath, Radhika's cousin. Our families would celebrate most of the festivals and holidays together. We also partied together. At one such party, I met Ambrish Srivastava and his wife Dolly. Ambrish and Rahul had been at IIT–BHU in Varanasi in the early 80s. Radhika and I became good friends with Ambrish and Dolly.

Vik was Dolly's younger brother. He was a portfolio manager in J. Goldman, and was covering technology stocks for the hedge fund. One day while we were still in Seattle, Ambrish called and said, 'My brother-in-law works as a portfolio manager in J. Goldman; you should meet him.' Vik and I met for lunch. Destiny wanted me to be a part of the world of Wall Street. Raheel Siddique suggested I become an analyst, Ambrish was an analyst and so was Vik in his early life. Vik then introduced me to Mark Mahaney, who gave me my first job on Wall Street.

13

INTERNET IS DEAD—LONG LIVE THE INTERNET

The Internet business saw a bull run between 1995 and 2000, followed by the big bust. By 2004, the good days returned. That's when Google went public.

Internet advertising was growing phenomenally. Google was growing so fast that Microsoft was forced to take countermeasures. Google and some other technology companies started talking about something called cloud computing in the discussions we had with them. They told us it would become huge in the years to come. It was becoming very clear that the world would be moving towards the Internet and with that, cloud computing and Internet advertising would be the way to make money rather than pre-installed software, which Microsoft made money from.

Cloud computing is when an individual or a company does not use its own computer storage space but hosts its data on third party web servers, and accesses it as and when required. The simplest example of cloud computing is Google's Gmail. Its users can access their files stored by Google via the Internet from any device. Like Google, Amazon also set up huge storage servers for their e-commerce business, which was growing at a steady pace. Eventually, the surplus storage space started being offered to other companies. Jeff Bezos also opened a subsidiary called Amazon Web Service, that focused purely on cloud computing.

While US companies were spreading their global dominance, far away in China, a company called Alibaba had taken roots. It was already well on its way to building a large Internet conglomerate. They got listed around the same time I joined Wall Street. The Internet sector was up and away once again. This time around, it was for ever and ever. In India, too, the Internet space had started unravelling and one of the first players in the e-commerce space was Indiaplaza.com. However, both India and China were probably a decade behind the US.

In the US, Apple was working on the iPhone, which would eventually change the way mobile phones were being used. This was the beginning of what would eventually become the smartphone age. The Internet was set to drive the world into an experience like never before.

FROM BIG CITI INTO A DARK TUNNEL

While I loved my job, what bothered me was that many of the analysts working with me had been at the same level for many years. I would have been forty by the time I was made senior analyst. One day I got a call from WR Hambrecht and they asked me to join them as senior Internet analyst. Somehow Mark got wind of this offer. He came by and said, 'I will be the happiest person when I see you as a senior analyst. However, I feel you should spend one more year here and then you will have a much stronger foundation.' I took his advice and continued with Citi. Mark is among the people who have shaped my career.

In May 2007, I quit Citi Group and joined as senior analyst in Oppenheimer.

In terms of size, Oppenheimer was nowhere close to Citi. Quite naturally, when Oppenheimer first contacted me, I said no. Shortly thereafter, I was talking to Bill Morris, a senior Internet analyst at another company. He knew that Oppenheimer had offered me a job, but I was not comfortable joining a smaller firm. He said, 'Do not make that mistake. Once you are a senior analyst, you are a senior analyst for the rest of your life. The size of the firm does not matter. Remember, you will never go back to becoming an associate analyst after that.' I knew what he was saying but found it difficult to accept it.

A few days passed in this state of indecision. One evening I was watching a film. Once it ended, the film credits started rolling. That's when it hit me. Being an associate analyst is like being an assistant director to the director of a movie. Many great movies have very talented assistant directors but the movie is always known for its director.

I decided to take the plunge.

For the first time in my life, I was working in a company that had only 800 employees. I was the only person there covering Internet companies, though. I had the authority to hire an associate analyst. I hired Stan Velikov, a Bulgarian. My association with Stan would continue for a fairly long time and across different companies, until I decided to leave Wall Street and start ShopClues.

I did quite well at Oppenheimer. Stan and I started bringing out some very significant research reports. Soon journalists from Bloomberg, ABC News, Fox News and other news channels started getting in touch with me to appear on TV and talk about Google, Yahoo and the Internet companies I covered. Internet was hot and I was basking in its glory.

Before coming to Oppenheimer, I would see me senior colleagues appearing on television all the time. Often I would prepare their notes for the shows. Naturally, I also had the desire to see myself on television.

TV: A NEW TURNING POINT

After joining Oppenheimer, I started carrying a suit, tie and formal shirt to the office in the hope that one day I would be called for a television show.

In May 2007, I got my chance. The appearance on CNBC was nerve-racking as well as overwhelming. I got a call requesting me to come to their studio. My throat started drying up as I made my way to the sets. Once I was inside the studio, everything around made me jumpy—the sound of the recording machine and the lights turning on and off.

As the appearances became regular, everything started feeling normal.

I felt completely out of depth during my first few interviews—not because of my command over the topics, but due to the lack of confidence in speaking in English on a live news show. I kept fumbling and stammering, but that just made me more determined to overcome my fears and become better at what I was doing. What I lacked in language abilities I more than made up for through the insights I presented to the viewers. I had the ability to connect the dots better than most other analysts of my time. While I came armed with operational insights into companies, other analysts looked simply at financial models and indulged in theoretical analysis.

My in-depth knowledge of the companies and my deep understanding of the changing Internet landscape in America made me a preferred choice for business news channels. Apart from CNBC, I appeared on FOX, ABC, Bloomberg and many other channels. On Fridays, when I worked from home, the television channels would send their mobile vans to my house for the live shows.

During the winter of 2007, Oppenheimer acquired CIBC World Market, a Canadian company. It later turned out to be a reverse merger. While Oppenheimer acquired CIBC, it gave CIBC's management team the control of the combined entity.

It was the first week of December. My boss called me and said they had decided to retain CIBC's Internet analyst, and needed to let me go. My world came crashing down. Would this be the end of my dreams? I held my nerves and decided to recover from one more setback. I had to start out yet again in the job market. However, within ten days of letting me go, my boss called and said, 'We want to hire you back.' While I was relieved to have my job back, things were not the same anymore. There was a lot of politicking. The Oppenheimer team did not see eye-to-eye with the CIBC folks. I worked there for the next four months, but by the end of March, I was told once again that I was being let go.

I immediately got in touch with a few head hunters I knew. Luckily, within a few days I got a call from a head hunter. He said, 'Collin Stewart, a UK-based company, is planning to expand their operations in the US and plan to hire an analyst.' The very next day I flew to New York to meet their senior management. At the meeting it was clear they knew about the situation at Oppenheimer and knew about their decision to let me go. I had confidence in my abilities and knew that I could deliver what they wanted. The meeting went off well and they promised to revert. Within an hour of the meeting, they called, wanting to make me an offer. I was thrilled. My annual package at Oppenheimer was $325,000, which was, quite frankly, a very decent salary. They asked about my expectation. I was jobless, yet I immediately said, '$550,000'. I somehow felt I had to go for broke.

Two hours later they called me back and the deal was sealed. I joined Collin Stewart. The first thing I did after joining was hire Stan as my associate. I started covering each and every Internet company, and not just the ones in Internet advertising, like I had been till then. By 2010, I was one of the top analysts in the business. I was the first analyst in the world to downgrade Google from a buy rating. My research said that Google was becoming a rich stock and there was no upside in the near term.

I was right. Google peaked at $800 and within six months after

I had downgraded it, the stock plummeted to $218. This was one of the best stock calls I made in my entire career. Soon I also became the first to downgrade eBay to a sell rating. I went straight from 'buy' to 'sell', bypassing the 'hold' rating. Many analysts considered it a very controversial call, but I was confident. eBay went from $30 to $10. I was right. Again.

RESEARCH, RESEARCH EVERYWHERE

Much of that research I did was poring over tonnes of data, white papers and annual reports. However, there was one aspect of my work as an analyst that helped me make certain pivotal decisions. One was that I was in networking. I attended dozens of industry conferences each year, and I tried to meet as many new people as I could during those events. I would pick their brain and that helped in building a perspective of how the industry was functioning. Most of the analysts primarily focused on the financial side of the companies but I had a lot of strategic insights.

I was the only Internet analyst who covered Microsoft; otherwise Microsoft was also covered by a software analyst. That helped me in building my reputation on Wall Street as an analyst. I knew that the world's largest software company would do anything to embrace the Internet. Their biggest challenger was Google, an Internet-born company. In 2008, I wrote a report on Microsoft in 2008 which became the industry spiller on why Microsoft was going after cloud computing and why Microsoft struggled to become a cloud service provider—services that would be delivered over the Internet.

There were several reasons why I downgraded Google. Google,

at that time, was a one-trick pony and all its revenue was coming from search. As they were dominating the market position, I expected regulatory pressure coming their way. Second, I noticed that all advertisers loved Google but it was becoming a monopolistic situation, which meant while there was not much option, all of them wanted another platform to be as powerful as Google. The third reason was the US market macroeconomy situation. I found that Google's internal budgeting was still discretionary. The fourth reason was that Google had taken a decision not to go after casino and healthcare-related keywords, which were very profitable businesses for Google. And the biggest reason was that Google was investing heavily in YouTube, Gmail, Chrome and Android, among other products, and it would remain in an investing mode for some time before all those new initiatives started making money.

My understanding of eBay was also not just based on theoretical research. eBay was one of the stocks that was at $10 when I started tracking it. I put a buy rating on eBay and said it would go up to $13. I thought it was overly beaten down. I realized that the initiatives eBay was working on were going to yield benefits in a very long term, and they had the problem of Amazon becoming stronger. eBay never acknowledged that; it never embraced fulfilment and delivery as a discipline. So I became the first analyst to put a sell rating on eBay.

Then I did a lot of research on how marketplaces function, things that they were doing to recover, how they were increasing their take rate and things they were doing with millions of small merchants. Once I was convinced, I changed my rating to buy on eBay. In my entire Wall Street career that call was my best call. eBay's stock went up from $10 to $44.

The years between 2008 and 2011 were a golden period, although most people consider this period as one of the worst phases in the financial world. This was the time when the Lehman Brothers collapsed and the crisis in the US economy had triggered a global economic meltdown. It was during this time that I made some critical decisions as an analyst and helped investors make a lot of money. I stayed with Collins Stewart from 2008 to 2010. In 2010, I joined Caris and Co., but by 2011, I had started feeling that I had done it all in this space. So, what next?

I resigned from Caris and Co. Next stop—ShopClues.

14

SHOPPING FOR CLUES

The first time I was bitten by the entrepreneurial bug was in 2001 when I was still pursuing MBA in the US. Towards the end of 2001, I created my first company, Korind, along with three friends in the 'land of opportunities'. The name of the company was a reflection of the ethnicity of the co-founders—three Indians and one South Korean.The US presidential elections had also drawn to a close, with George Bush defeating Al Gore. In those days, Indo–US relationships had been strengthened further on account of the significant outsourcing of a large number of business processes to India. Korind was set up with an aim to capitalize on the need in the US market to reduce costs by setting up Business Process Outsourcing (BPO) units in India. Our business was to help US companies find suitable outsourcing partners in India. We wanted to ride the next big wave in the field of information technology.

When I look back, it was quite a gamble. I was just two-years-old in the US and that too, on a student loan. All I should have done was study and do well in the MBA programme. But perhaps the fire in my belly always made my try that little bit more. While I was building Korind, I had no training and no money, but I had ambition, desire and capability.

All four of us—Amit Khetan, Aaron Kim, Amitabh Nagpal and I—chipped in $1000 each to start the company. Amit and I were in the US on student visas, hence we could not create a company on our own. Since Amitabh was a green card holder and Aaron Kim was an American citizen, they were given the task of incorporating the company. However, except for Amit Khetan and me, the other two had very little time to spare for the fledgling venture.

We had started the company after 9/11. This was a time when George Bush was trying to revive the economy from the aftermath of the catastrophic events. One of the ways to make US businesses more profitable was to outsource some of the business processes to a country where the manpower costs were low. It became abundantly clear that outsourcing was the next big thing in the relations between the US and India. We wanted to help American businesses outsource some of their processes to India and find them the right partners to work with.

Korind would have grown a lot more if only the four of us had more time for it, but it did make some money. The venture still remains very close to my heart—not only because it was my first company, but also because it helped me understand the basics of business.

VENTURING CAPITAL

Every day that I spent working as a financial analyst was with one objective: creating enough nest eggs so I could eventually plunge full-time as an entrepreneur. Simultaneously, I kept on working on a business plan. Towards the end of 2007, I felt I was ready to fly solo. For months I had worked on readying a pitch for venture capital firms, so they would agree to back my plan to launch a bunch of online portals under the umbrella of Clues Network, with sub-brands like DealClues, FinanceClues, Travel Clues, ShoppingClues, AdmissionClues and InvestmentClues.

I made my first presentation to Vispi Daver of Sierra Ventures and Sumir Chadha of Sequoia Ventures. This was also my first articulation of an idea of what would eventually become ShopClues. I was very naïve in the beginning as I had very little understanding of the working of venture funds, but I was a fast learner. With Sequoia giving some very positive signals, I got the confidence of pitching my idea to other venture capitalists.

Then tragedy struck in the form of a global financial meltdown triggered by the collapse of the Lehman Brothers. Sequoia pulled back and so did the others. Sequoia even made a presentation with the title 'Rest in Peace', which meant there would be no investments in startups.

I had no option but to park my ideas aside and hope the economy would get back on track.

A LITTLE BIT OF CHINA IN INDIA

In August 2010, the Indian online travel portal MakeMyTrip (MMYT) got listed on the US bourses. It was a historic moment for Internet companies in India, as it gave wings to many ambitious entrepreneurs. Listing a company on the bourses is also a validation of its success.

Vik and a few of my other friends, who were also Wall Street analysts with various financial services companies, kept talking endlessly about this development and how it had opened up new opportunities in India's Internet space. They egged me on to grab this opportunity and start covering Indian companies. Their argument was simple—being an Indian, I could offer unique insights into the workings of the Internet-driven companies in India.

Vik was right. I had to look no further than within the company to see the success of China-born analyst Jason Brueschke, who covered Chinese stocks for Citi. Jason was an example of why someone from a particular country would have a much better understanding of not only the companies and their financial performances but also the demographics, culture and consumer behaviour in the country.

I started working on my coverage plan of MMYT. At that time I covered very large stocks like Google, Yahoo and Amazon that were worth between $13 billion and $15 billion. Compared to these companies, MMYT's market capitalization was less than $1 billion. During my entire career as an analyst, I never followed the norm among analysts to write simple one-page reports with a 'buy' or 'sell' rating. I decided to write my first report on India—'Has India Internet finally arrived'.

I was of the firm belief that India was different. Even though the Internet was 17 years old, very little was happening in this space in India beyond instant messaging, WhatsApp, porn downloads and Google Search. I wrote a 35-page detailed report on the Indian Internet industry and how it was shaping up, ending with why someone should invest in MMT. In comparison, the Internet market had already crossed $200 billion for US companies. Americans were using the Internet for numerous things, from travel to DVD rentals to buying a laptop or a mobile phone, and much more. At that time, no one really cared about India's Internet potential. That was for a reason. Before MMYT there was only one Indian company—SIFY—that traded on Nasdaq. SIFY's low market capitalization of $50 million was nothing to write home about.

I visited India within the next couple of months to get a feel of how things were on the ground. Apart from Deep Kalra and Rajesh Magow of MMYT, I also met entrepreneurs of other companies—Pearl Uppal of Fashion and You, Quikr's CEO Pranay Chulet, Vinay Gupta of Via travel portal and Dhruv Shringi of Yatra, among fifteen other company founders and CEOs.

It was during this visit that I realized that for all practical purposes, the Indian market was just taking baby steps in the Internet business.

INDIA AND AMERICA

I decided to go back to the US and plan the jump into India's e-commerce space. However, there was one hitch—I had no idea how to tackle the technology part. An Internet company without a unique technology play was impossible. That is when I thought of Row9, a technology company run by two of my friends—Ned Taylor and Lawrence Kosick—and offered to buy their technology platform. Mrinal Chatterjee, the vice president of engineering at Row9, who eventually became the vice president of engineering at ShopClues, would be a part of the discussions with Row9. Initially, they agreed, but the deal didn't go through. Finally, I decided to outsource the technology work to Wiantech, which was based in India. At that time, the company was to be called DealClues.

The initial days of building up the technology were difficult. I had a day job which demanded total and undivided attention. In the evenings, I worked with Wiantech to build the technology platform. I was an entrepreneur from 6 p.m. to 12 p.m. After roughly 3.5 hours of sleep, I was up and back to being a research assistant. This went on for more than a month.

This was also the time when websites offering deals were mushrooming all over and shutting down in equal measure. Mine was not a deal-seeking site, hence I decided to change the name from DealClues to ShoppingClues. Then ShoppingClues got shortened to ShopClues on 7 January 2011.

Later, in January, I visited India for the second time on being asked to speak at the VCCircle E-Commerce Conference. It was at the event that I happened to meet my future rivals—Sachin Bansal and Binny Bansal of Flipkart as well as Kunal Bahl of Snapdeal. These three individuals were already the poster boys of Indian startups by then. I also met Google India's Rajan Anandan, who was hugely appreciative of my Indian Internet report. He and I were the two keynote speakers at the conference.

While interacting with the Indian startups, I realized that an inventory-led model wouldn't work in India in the long run. So I decided to create India's first pure-play e-marketplace. Marketplace, like the name, suggests a platform where a large number of sellers can come and sell their products.

On the flight back to the US, I dreamt up a plan and it was so exciting that it kept me awake through the entire 15-hour flight. I even wrote the detailed business requirements for ShopClues. The fundamentals of my future business had been written on an airplane.

I could not wait for the plane to land. The moment it did, I called the Wiantech guys to make a bunch of changes to the technology. I also started working on the ShopClues logo on my own and what I created then remained the company's logo for the first three years.

In February I came to know of an off-price retail conference in Las Vegas. Companies would come and sell their last year's unsold goods at an ultra-low cost. I had a few visiting cards printed and met the brand heads of many of the participating companies. These meeting helped me understand how to buy goods at very low cost and sell them for a profit.

Simultaneously, I started talking to my friends in Silicon Valley and began working on an investor deck, which is the most important aspect of fundraising. First I met Vinod Dham, founder of Indo–US Venture Partners. He was known as Intel's 'Pentium Engineer'. Vinod's own journey is like folklore in Silicon Valley. Born in Pune, he arrived in the US with just $8 and worked very hard on his way to becoming one of the most successful people in the world of technology.

Vinod told me that I should meet his team in India. Vani Kola, who heads Kalaari Capital now, was working with Vinod then. I met her in Bengaluru (then Bangalore). I was extremely nervous because it had been a long time since I had made a formal pitch to a VC firm. The last had been when I had made a pitch to Sequoia and

Sierra. Vani ripped my presentation apart. Radhika and Mrinal—who had joined the meeting through a video conference—were absolutely stunned. Vinod was both unhappy and embarrassed. It was a weird situation.

Clearly, I had made a terrible presentation and had failed miserably in communicating my vision of an e-marketplace clearly. Another reason why I failed was perhaps Vani felt I was not committed about moving back to India. Vinod was magnanimous enough to give me another chance. 'I am happy to take another look but after you have moved back to India,' he said.

I went back and decided to take a break. We spent a few days at some of the fanciest beach resorts in LA, but for shopping we went to off-price retailers and indulged in binge-buying.

15

BABY STEPS

I met Arun Sagar at a sports club near my house. Both of us loved playing squash and soon we became good friends. A rocket scientist, Arun was among the first employees of Microsoft and knew a lot about technology. By then I had already selected a standard technology platform. Arun helped in uploading the technology software I had decided upon onto Godaddy.com. That day he created the first-ever version of ShopClues.com. We took pictures of the stuff I had bought in LA—Joseph Abboud cufflinks, DKNY watches and Mark Jacob wallets—and uploaded them from the backend. Even though I was seeing the same images at the frontend on the website, it felt great.Our business was that of a marketplace, so we had to take extra care towards the ease of listing on the website for merchants.

Our initial focus was to get the feedback from customers and merchants so we could improve. We had to offer a lot of autonomy to the sellers, unlike platforms like Flipkart, which at the time had an inventory-based model. Flipkart would buy the products, list them on their website and sell them at a price of their choosing. More often than not, the sale price would be lower than the purchase price.

As a reaction to this trend, the Government of India introduced regulations that made it mandatory for e-commerce companies to operate as e-marketplaces only. The government feared that e-commerce companies would offer huge discounts that would adversely affect India's offline retailers. In the marketplace model, any retailer will be free to list their products on e-commerce platforms. Flipkart pivoted to a marketplace but created WS Retail to go around the regulation. WS Retail soon became the largest seller on Flipkart.

ShopClues remained a true marketplace. We wanted the seller to easily upload product information without our intervention. We also figured ways to make it simple for sellers to change the prices of their products that were already listed on the site. As I kept thinking of more scenarios, the complexities increased. The list of thirty features increased to fifty, sixty and beyond.

One day I was sitting in my office and recalling my interaction with Vani, and her trashing my business model. All of a sudden, my cellphone rang and an unknown number flashed on the screen. I thought of disconnecting, but reluctantly took the call.

'Hey, Sandeep, this is Chaim Friedman from Starlims,' said the person. Starlims Technologies was a laboratory information management system firm, which had recently gone public. Chaim was the chief financial officer of Starlims and his elder brother Itschak was the CEO. Oppenheimer had advised them during the IPO. One of the reasons why Oppenheimer had hired me as a senior analyst was because they had an IPO mandate for this company and they had to make sure they had a research analyst who could cover this company.

'I don't know if you kept track of Starlims, but we sold the company to Abbott Laboratories three years after listing it on Nasdaq,' he said. Honestly, I hadn't kept track of Starlims. Chaim added, 'Your research coverage was amazing and you made great calls on eBay and Amazon, and your research notes on Microsoft and Google were very good. We thought of connecting with you and telling you that my brother and I now run a venture capital fund, and it would be great if we could collaborate in some manner... We can give you the capital, you can keep some equity and run the company,' Chaim said.

There was my opportunity. I immediately pitched ShopClues to him. My heart was pumping and I was trying desperately to disguise my lack of confidence. The Vani Kola meeting had damaged me more than I had imagined. 'How much money are you looking for?' Chaim asked.

'One to 1.5 million,' I replied.

'Let me speak with Itschak and call you back,' he said.

Two hours later both the brothers called and asked, 'What's the valuation you have in mind?'

Honestly, I hadn't given valuation any serious thought till then. '$5 million is what I am looking at,' I said instinctively.

'We would like to invest $600,000... You can go and tell others that you have secured some funds... Let's finalize the documents,' Chaim said.

I couldn't believe I had just secured almost half the amount

I needed to start ShopClues. I couldn't control my excitement and immediately called up Radhika to share the news. Lady luck had finally smiled on us. Over the next few weeks, I met a few more investors and secured another $1 million. The baby was ready to run.

However, destiny had planned something else for me, as I realized later.

GETTING KNOCKED DOWN AGAIN

During fundraising I had written to dozens of venture capitalists. One of them was Kleiner Perkins. Ajit Nazre, one of the partners at Kleiner Perkins, got in touch with me and we met a few times, not long after I had secured the initial funds.

When I met Perkins I already had a commitment of $1.6 million from a couple of angel investors. Perhaps that is also why Kleiner Perkins got interested. VCs start liking you more when you already have an offer in hand.

Ajit wanted to meet the ShopClues team. By then, Mrinal was already on board. I didn't want to give them the impression that ours was a family business and hence I took everyone except Radhika along. All of us went to Kleiner Perkins' office on Sandhill Road.

The meeting, which was attended by a few other senior partners, went on for three hours. Sherpalo Ventures ran Kleiner Perkins' India operations and Sandeep Murthy from Sherpalo dialled in for a phone conference. After the meeting, Ajit took me aside and said that the meeting had been good and that he would call me in the next couple of days.

Sanjay Sethi was also part of the ShopClues dream by then,

although he was yet to quit eBay and I hadn't quit Caris. It was decided that Sanjay and I would go to meet Sandeep. We took the next day's flight to Mumbai. Before leaving the US, I designed two business cards with the ShopClues logo. I emailed them to a friend whose father stayed in Mumbai and requested his dad to get the cards printed and delivered to ITC's Grand Central hotel, which was where we had booked ourselves.

We arrived in Mumbai the next day, took our cards, bought six bottles of Corona and went straight to meet Sandeep Murthy. When I gave Sandeep the business card, he had a smile on his face. I told him during the meeting that Radhika would be heading the marketing and merchandising for the company. The meeting went off fabulously well. Sanjay headed back to the US the next day and I went to Baroda, where Radhika was vacationing with the kids. After a long time things were picking up. We were ecstatic.

They liked the clarity around a managed marketplace. They loved my background as an Internet analyst. They knew about me—thanks to Mary Meeker. She was also one of the most sought-after Internet analysts, and had joined Kleiner Perkins that year. Mary and I were contemporaries as analysts who had attended many analyst calls together. That helped.

What really worked? My pitch was clear. I wanted to offer those categories that were not sold by the current crop of e-commerce players in India. There was a need to organize the non-standard categories. Ram Shriram (who had sold his company to Amazon) knew that well. Amazon was not strong in softline retail. I also explained the importance of going to tier-II and tier-III markets. The pitch was compelling.

For Kleiner Perkins, it was important to go ahead with a

meaningful investment in India, which they didn't have then.

The offer on the table was of $5 million. They knew that I was raising $1.6 million at $5 million valuation. I was giving away 30 per cent in equity. Kleiner Perkins wanted to invest $5 million at a valuation of $7 million.

Ajit called while I was still in Baroda. He sounded quite upbeat. 'Once you get a term sheet from us, it is like getting admission in Harvard University,' he said. A term sheet is the letter of intent of investment but is a non-binding document. But what really matters for startups are term sheets, because that shows that a venture capitalist likes your concept, your vision, your business plan and has agreed to invest money in your business.

In the next one-and-a-half months, Kleiner Perkins sent me the term sheet. Thereafter, we started finalizing all the documentation needed from our end. However, I soon realized that there had been no further communication from Kleiner Perkins. I asked my attorney, Anil Advani, what was next. He said, 'Close the deal.'

By now we had decided to relocate to India in August. We even had our kids admitted to a school in India.

I kept chasing Ajit and he kept giving evasive answers. He would give me a different reason for the delay every time I called. Once he even said that Flipkart had already become a $1 billion company and they were figuring out the right valuation for ShopClues, and on another occasion he said that Amazon was planning to enter India.

I decided to call Ajit one last time. I asked him straight out, 'Are you guys giving me the money? Yes or no?' He avoided a direct reply yet again. I had my answer. But there was no looking back. We sold off everything and were ready to move back to India.

SHOPCLUES' FUTURE CEO

The first time I met Sanjay Sethi was in November 2010. It was during my son's birthday. He had come to drop his daughter off to my home for the birthday gathering. His daughter and my son went to the same school.

That day I got introduced to him. He was with eBay, so he knew about me as an analyst. But it was really funny that he didn't know that I was Sandeep Aggarwal. There was an awkward moment—I had downgraded eBay's stocks, even though later I gave it a buy rating, at least three quarters before an upgrade from entire Wall Street. In the months to come we became fonder of each other and started hanging around. April onwards, he started visiting us more often. Sometimes he would come and grab a couple of beers at my place, and we would spend our time talking about ShopClues and the e-commerce landscape in India.

I knew that he was willing to venture out. But for the longest time there was no discussion of him joining the company. I was also not sure if I should bring in a partner from outside. On hindsight, I shouldn't have done that.

So just before the meeting with Kleiner Perkins, Sanjay Sethi came on board. For the meeting I was also in touch with Mrinal Chatterjee, who was the vice president of engineering at ShopClues. I knew that it was important to show that I had good talent along with me. It was an important meeting.

Eventually, when I was not there in the company, Radhika and Sanjay Sethi were the oldest team members. That helped when we had to choose a CEO for the company who wasn't a family member.

A LIFELINE

The last twenty days in the US were frenetic. From everything I had gone to nothing, again. I went back to Chaim Friedman and told him about the Kleiner Perkins episode. Chaim said that his offer was still the same, of $600,000. That was a huge relief. Over the next few days, I met more VCs and investors than ever before.

I finally raised $1.95 million from sixteen of my friends, including Chaim. Those twenty-odd days tested the limits of my staying power and I was emotionally and physically drained by the time I headed back to India. Despite the anxiety and stress of launching myself into the entrepreneurial orbit, I was extremely happy and satisfied at what I had achieved till then.

On 25 August 2011, after twelve years in the US, I, for the first time, bought a one-way ticket to India. I was leaving the US for good. The country where I had bought my first house, my first car and the country which I had never thought I would leave, and where I had thought my children would grow up. As the airplane took off, I said a final goodbye.

Radhika and the kids were there to receive me at the Delhi airport. India looked different, smelt different, felt different. Over the last twelve years, I had visited India like a tourist. This time around I was back as an Indian. I noticed a lot more about India and I also compared India a lot more with the US. The dirt along the roads, the number of stray animals, the nightmarish traffic and the oppressive heat had suddenly become issues that were bothersome. India was the same as before, but I had changed.

Radhika had already finalized a house in Gurugram (then Gurgaon) and so had Sanjay. Mrinal was iffy about moving to India after Kleiner Perkins backed out, but eventually he also moved back to India and rented a house in Gurugram.

Soon ShopClues found its first office. Years later, the same office also became Droom's first office. This office has been lucky for me and the startups I have started.

16

PERILS OF A TOURIST

When I left this country many years ago I never thought that I would come back for good. But here I was. The India I had left twelve years ago and the India I had come back to were very similar, and yet, different. Things still moved at a very slow pace, but for businesses across the world, India was on its way to again becoming an economic power—it was being seen as a land of golden opportunities. I was no longer a tourist in my own country and was here to start a new journey. I felt happy. I was ready for a new life in Gurgaon a swish satellite on the outskirts of Delhi, which was also India's second Silicon Valley

(Bangalore being the first). Companies like MakeMyTrip, Snapdeal and Yatra had already set shop in Gurugram. Delhi was home to the czars of the old economy, people like Sunil Mittal, the Modis and the Birlas. Gurgaon had been adopted by those who had started making a mark in 'new' India.

Gurugram offered the comfort and safety of living in a gated community, with all the amenities that we had in the US—a gym, a health club, a squash court and a swimming pool.

THE WINTER CHILL

In 2007, when I was still considering the idea of starting-up in India, I made a trip back home. I stayed with a friend, Amitabh Nagpal, in Gurgaon. He was the country manager of a leading MNC. 'You will get everything here that you get in the US,' he told me. I was sceptical then. But six months before I moved back to India, Radhika and I spent some days in Gurgaon to get a feel of the city. I was impressed with what Gurgaon had to offer.

I had considered starting up in Bangalore too. After all, it was the startup hub of the country. I even thought of Mumbai, it being the financial capital. I had my own reasons to finally choose Gurgaon. Amitabh's lifestyle made me believe that Gurgaon would be a soft landing for my family. Another important factor was that hiring talent would be easier, since there were a lot of technology companies here. I even knew some of the startup founders in Gurgaon personally. Asking for their help, if needed, would be easier. The icing on the cake was that a few of my friends from the US had also settled down in Gurgaon. The last reason that finally made us choose Gurgaon was that two of my main team members had their parents living in Delhi.

THE PIGEONHOLE

To realize your dreams you need to make sacrifices. I had sacrificed plenty—a high-paying job, frequent television appearances as a Wall Street analyst, a lot of money and a jolly good life in the US. However, India offered a dream that no other country did. The opportunity to build India's first true e-commerce marketplace was just too good to let go. If the same opportunities existed in Siberia or Uganda, I would've gone there too.

I wanted to be a pioneer. An e-marketplace is an online platform which allows merchants to sell their products online directly. Amazon and Flipkart, too, run marketplaces now, but they also have their own proxy retailers selling on their site.

Planning a company and setting one up are completely different. We had some surprises awaiting us. The contractor chosen to do our office's interiors took a fat advance and disappeared without finishing the work. This was my first expensive lesson in running a business—don't trust people easily. But what when people who are already within your 'circle of trust' betray you?

Anyway, I had to be frugal unlike some of the other entrepreneurs of that time. I couldn't squander money just because it was not mine. I started with finding an office where I did not have to pay a lot in rent. A childhood friend, Vipin Gupta, whom I had not met for almost 30 years, came as a godsend. His father was dad's colleague in Karnal. Even though he had lived in Gurgaon for years and knew the place like the back of his hand, I was reluctant to ask for his help. My father spoke to him without telling me. Vipin called one day and said, 'There is this guy... he has an office here, a very beaten-down place, but you can take a look if you want to.'

Having worked in the fanciest offices in the US, including Microsoft, I also dreamt of something similar, and Gurgaon had plenty of swanky office buildings. But I couldn't afford extravagance. I decided that I wanted a place that would be welcoming to employees as well as visitors, a place that would breed innovation, a place that would set the benchmark in creation of talent.

Vipin and I went to see this office. It was an old, somewhat unplanned building. The landlord showed me a large hall on the top floor. The glasses were broken, pigeons were flying around inside, there were layers of dust on the floor and, to top it all, there were beehives. I made up my mind to decline the place. Then the landlord showed me the basement—I didn't know till then there was one. The moment he showed me the basement, everything changed. Suddenly, the rusty building had transformed into an office inside my head. I would have my office on the top floor and use the basement as a warehouse to pack and fulfil the orders.

I bargained hard and got the building at a fifth of the cost of what the other fancy properties would have cost me. I then spent Rs 10 lakh ($15,000) renovating the building. Even after so many years of being there—earlier when it was the ShopClues office and now when it is home to Droom—it is still very affordable in terms of rent. I have now taken the entire building. Those days I hand-picked every single piece of furniture we needed. While the office was getting renovated, I also planned how the fulfilment would happen. I was not going to waste any time. The clock was ticking for the launch of my venture.

I was not an engineer, but I was very good in building processes. I designed a plan for how the goods would arrive at the warehouse, how they'd be inspected, how they'd be packed and, finally, dispatched.

THE MILK RUN

We were the world's first marketplace to offer fulfilment service from the very first day of operation. I was a firm believer that it was important to build a platform that encouraged small and medium sellers, who didn't have the capability to pack and ship items.

Logistics in India was patchy at best. For e-commerce companies, timely and safe delivery was becoming the new battlefield. Companies like Flipkart and Snapdeal had decided to spend millions of dollars to spruce up the delivery arm by setting up their own logistics network to address this problem. Services like same-day-delivery and next-day-delivery had also begun to find traction.

Here we were, in our small little office, trying to outwit the big guys. We were perhaps not as quick as them, but we were doing things right. We called it milk run—the last mile pick-up. When a customer purchased an item on ShopClues, the very next morning we would pick up the merchandise from the seller, bring it to our fulfilment centre, inspect it, match it with the order, generate a receipt, pack it in a ShopClues box, tape it and ship it.

Our top management team comprised Mrinal, vice president of engineering; Radhika, vice president of marketing and Sanjay Sethi, vice president of operations. All three reported to me.

ACQUIRING TALENT

We soon hired Devesh Rai as vice president of business development. He had graduated from IIM Calcutta and had worked with large multinationals. He was perhaps the sharpest person in ShopClues hired by me.

Our last meeting before he joined us was at a hotel in Gurgaon. I was not sure if I wanted to take him to our small office. I thought he would see this beaten-down place and turn down our offer. With a lot of trepidation, I said, 'Devesh, I have finalized our office space. Would you like to see it?'

He jumped at the idea and we drove down together. He saw the office and smiled. He told me later that after seeing the office, his respect for my style of work increased significantly. 'There are very few entrepreneurs who know how to stay frugal,' he told me. Devesh was a person who really cared about the best use of financial resources.

THE 17-YEAR-OLD INDUSTRY

In 2012, e-commerce in India was already a 17-year-old industry, but for all practical purposes, it was still taking infant steps.

Even then, Flipkart was the big daddy of Indian e-commerce. But theirs was largely an inventory-led model. It bought the goods from wholesalers at a bargain, stocked them at their warehouses and shipped them as and when an order was received. The law at the time said MNCs couldn't invest in retail, hence the government banned e-commerce companies to operate as retailers, but allowed them to operate as marketplaces.

As a consequence, Flipkart pivoted to become a marketplace. But in a rather strange and suspect manner, they set up WS Retail and made it a seller on Flipkart. Essentially, Flipkart used WS Retail as its proxy seller.

There were about six–seven large e-commerce companies at the time. Indian e-commerce demographics were also very different. Of the 80 million Internet users in India at the time, only two million shopped online. Without calculating discounts and promotions, the gross sale of the entire industry was about $200 million. Except ShopClues, all other companies had an inventory-based model. Hence, they wasted a lot of money on marketing, promoted cash-on-delivery and never dared to charge for shipping. I had a dramatically different opinion. I was of the view that for an online company to become a retail giant in a place like India, it couldn't be done through an inventory-led model. The only option was an e-marketplace. I thought there could never be a Walmart-like company in the retail space in India, and no company could become that big through just physical outlets.

My belief was vindicated when Walmart decided to pick up 77 per cent stake in Flipkart for $16 billion—making it the largest e-commerce deal in the world. There were reasons. India is all about small traders. There are about 15–20 million small and medium entrepreneurs. Most of them make products in non-standard categories and offer a long list of products. I could not see how an inventory-based model could offer 40 million products in its catalogue and give buyers the depth and breadth of the categories they wanted. If all these products could not reach the buyers, an inventory-led model was bound to fail. Also, the cost of buying and maintaining inventory was very high. I was very clear in my mind—my competition was neither Flipkart nor Snapdeal.

AN ANALYST'S HAT

When I was in the US, I had to watch every move of eBay and Amazon as part of my job. I knew exactly why Amazon and eBay lost the China battle. I knew their strengths and weaknesses. I also knew that when e-commerce became a little more sizeable in India, Amazon would make its entry. Once that happened, it would change the market completely.

Amazon invented the standard categories game and it's impossible to beat them at their own game. In categories like books, electronics, mobiles and computers, they know how to go for the kill. I wanted to safeguard ShopClues from Amazon's entry. From Day One, I was clear that ShopClues should create dominance in a space that doesn't overlap with Amazon. Hence, we went after the sellers in second and third tier towns, which I perceived would be Amazon's weakness.

THE 35TH ENTRANT

The market of horizontal e-commerce, companies who would sell almost everything, was a cluttered market at that time. ShopClues became the 35th entrant into the e-commerce space, but it was the first in a few important things. We were the first managed marketplace, which implies that we offered fulfilment services, and that too, from Day One. We were also the first to offer a common return policy. The first to offer a payment escrow to ensure that a buyer's money remained safe if anything went wrong with the seller's product. These three things would define our existence. These differentiators also made us grow phenomenally.

One part of my strategy was to understand what Amazon and Flipkart were doing and move ShopClues away from direct competition with them. The other crucial part of my strategy was to make a mark in the market we wanted to dominate.

I never liked cash-on-delivery. So I came up with the concept called Clues Bucks, something like loyalty points. However, a ShopClues buyer would earn Clues Bucks only for a prepaid transaction. For those who ordered in exchange for cash-on-delivery, there would be no loyalty points. That didn't mean I stopped cash-on-delivery. How could I? Eighty per cent of the market was cash-on-delivery. I incentivized customers against it, and within the first year, cash-on-delivery on ShopClues dropped to a mere 8 per cent of the total orders.

As for fulfilment services to the sellers, I called it ShopClues Velocity. I also gave our sellers choice. There were three versions of the service: ShopClues Velocity Premium, ShopClues Velocity Basic and Merchant Direct Fulfilment.

ANYTHING FOR BUSINESS

I was ready to meet anyone who sold anything for a living. Everyone was a potential seller. It did not matter what they sold.

Around the time, I went to a party hosted by my friend Ranjeet Oak (who is the chief revenue officer at MakyMyTrip). There I met this gentleman who dealt with Swiss army brands in India. I told him about ShopClues. 'Why don't you sell your products on ShopClues?' I asked him. He was immediately interested. Soon, we went to his office to catalogue their products. That was how we had our first seller going live with his products.

There was another person—we called him Jain Sahib—who had sold us office laptops, computers and printers. He had a shop called Jain Computers. One day I went to his shop and saw a big room full of printers. I asked him if he would like to sell the printers on

ShopClues. At that time none of the small traders had any idea about how to sell goods online. Jain Sahib knew about Flipkart, but did not know he could also sell online. 'Jain Sahib, if you sell through my platform, even when your shop is closed, someone could still buy your products,' I explained to him.

Mr Jain's wife was an engineer. She helped him in the business. I asked if I could meet him and his wife. We met and I explained everything I knew about e-commerce to them. They decided to give us a chance to sell their inventory. My team put Jain Sahib's entire inventory online. Similarly, we visited innumerable small stores and created their catalogues ourselves.

We also landed some big sellers—The Elephant Company and the Bombay Store.

17

THE INDIA WAY

ShopClues went live on 21 November 2011, but only on Facebook. By then FB had overtaken Google's Orkut to become the world's new Internet sensation as well as a social media giant. Anyone who understood the power and relevance of social media had a Facebook account. It was considered unsexy if you weren't there. Hence, it made perfect sense to launch ourselves on Facebook.The number of online shoppers in 2011 was only two million, which was actually a very small buyer base. However, I read India differently. We were where China was in 2003 or the US was in 1995. India was at the cusp of breaking out. Most of the online shoppers in 2011 were either doing it because of the convenience it offered or for getting a good bargain. This meant that people were either buying completely standardized items or cheap products. I was of the view that e-commerce buyers were still *not* ready to spend Rs 3,000 for a shirt or Rs 10,000 for a piece of furniture. However, one item that was selling massively was phones. I believe that the sales of electronic items led to the e-commerce boom in India, much like what books had done for the US.

But where there is an opportunity, can conmen be far behind? Some buyers ended up receiving a brick in a neatly wrapped box instead of a phone. Every time we blacklisted such sellers, they tried their best to come back under a different name. I remember writing a blog about getting cheated by sellers. There's no way to tell exactly how many fakes were on our platform, but I do accept that as startup companies, not only ShopClues, everyone made a lot of mistakes.

It was also a time when returns and logistics services weren't apt. And the fact that cash-on-delivery was the most-preferred option made things far from ideal. Flipkart flourished on cash payments, hence everyone else felt compelled to copy their model.

Even at the time I was launching ShopClues, I knew that sooner rather than later Amazon and Alibaba—two of the world's largest e-commerce companies—would enter India and become dominant players. While I was at ShopClues, I did everything to differentiate us from the other players in order to survive and thrive. Unfortunately, many e-commerce players lost the plot when they started playing the game the way the bigger players wanted them to play it. Instead of focusing on their USPs, they wanted to outlast the behemoths in this fight. Result: ShopClues and Snapdeal have been reduced to insignificance. Walmart-owned Flipkart and Amazon have ended up burying all the other players. But that was not how it was supposed to unfold.

During the time I headed ShopClues, I had dug trenches and was ready for their onslaught. My entire plan was based on the fact that India was different from the US or China. I decided that ShopClues would focus on non-branded products and small sellers. Amazon's strength was in selling books, electronics and computers, fulfilled by large sellers. I did the opposite.

We looked at items which had demand among tier-II users. We did not sell them a Rs 5,000 Bugatti perfume, but we would sell them a Rs 250 unbranded or lesser-known branded perfume. We didn't sell them Nike t-shirts for Rs 2000 but we sold them Rs 160 t-shirts, which resembled the Nike ones.

Smaller towns had several cost-conscious digital-centric users. So we bought keywords to drive traffic not from Delhi, Mumbai, or Bangalore, but for Kota in Rajasthan, Coimbatore, etc. We bought keywords and geo-targeted tier-II and tier-III cities for the products.

The plan was watertight; we never pivoted, never changed, never deferred from what I presented to Kleiner Perkins in June 2011. For the next five years our strategy remained the same.

We finally launched beta version, where the shopper had to like our page on Facebook in order go on to Shopclues.com. This system went on until 29 May 2012.

Many questioned the logic of launching on Facebook. It was quite simple, actually: I did not want to spend money on advertising on print, radio or TV. We were an online platform that wanted online users, hence, the best way was to become visible through online platforms. Interestingly, we were one of the first companies in the e-commerce space to use the power of the social media to propel ourselves. The idea was to be as frugal as possible.

THE HIRING CONUNDRUM

Building the core team emerged as my biggest problem. The people who were the right fit asked for top dollar. Some of them had spent 12–15 years in the US. Indian startups hadn't yet become fancied in the job market. During one interview I met a 26-year-old boy. He was getting married soon and was looking for a job that would pay more than the multinational he was working for. He rejected our offer, saying, 'My in-laws haven't heard about ShopClues and are not happy with the idea of me working for an unknown entity.'

Young people preferred working with companies like Infosys and Wipro, or the multinationals. They wanted offices that looked as swanky as Google or Facebook. We operated almost like a bootstrapped startup and hardly anyone in India understood how such startups operate. In India, all potential employees could only judge the company by analysing the facilities and infrastructure it offered. People wanted to get assurance that we were a legitimate company and not some fly-by-night operator.

Luckily for us, that was the time when consolidation had started happening in the e-commerce space. When Flipkart bought LetsBuy, one of their founders reached out to us for a job. Of course, I was delighted. I also figured that if Flipkart wasn't retaining LetsBuy's employees, it was an opportunity for us to hire. We camped at LetsBuy's office. At that point, there were only 25–30 vacancies but we ended up hiring 70 people!

PROBLEMS IN THE NORTHEAST

It was exciting when we saw a lot of initial demand from the Northeast—Meghalaya, Assam, Manipur and Nagaland. Our portfolio of products was unique and different as well as cheap and durable. At the time, nobody was catering to this market. Potential customers wrote to us saying they wanted goods delivered to their doorstep. We tried a lot of courier companies but realized that most of them were not catering to a majority of the pin codes in the Northeast. We started using India Post, the Indian government's postal service, which delivered letters and parcels to the remotest village in every part of India. Online customers were unforgiving. They wanted to pay the least possible amount for the products and also wanted the perfect experience. There were times when I would personally call, if an order would get wrongly delivered, to apologize. That didn't help much, though. If orders got delayed, we were ridiculed. For example, if someone had pre-paid for a product, if we did not ship it within two days, they would immediately conclude someone had run away with their money. Some people thought we were also out to scam customers. Every time something went wrong, we gave the customer a refund or sent him a new product. Sometimes even that wouldn't help.

The delivery problem was acute in the Northeast and we started losing a lot of money because of delivery issues. We tried hard but finally most of my team members wanted to withdraw from there. I remained reluctant for six–seven months, but finally, even I gave up.

A couple of years later, things changed when courier companies became more efficient and accountable, but by then we had lost the opportunity of being kings of that market. Soon, the Northeast became an important destination for all other e-commerce companies.

CUSTOMER AT THE CENTRE

E-commerce is a customer-centric business—Amazon showed the world how to build a customer-centric business. That was outlined in Amazon's CEO, Jeff Bezos' first letter to its stakeholder.

I did not want to build an Amazon copy, but ShopClues had to become nothing short of an Indian Amazon when it came to customer and seller centricity. We started with a clearly defined seller policy. We also built a seller and merchant central, which detailed out the Dos and Don'ts of becoming a seller on ShopClues.

Counterfeit was a big problem. It was important to stop merchants from selling duplicate items. Some merchants sold refurbished products at the price of new products. They did not disclose that these products were used, and offered heavy discounts on them.

Sometimes we were harsh on our sellers. At times we also took legal action. One of it was to suspend the seller for a week on the first violation, two weeks on the second and for a month on the third.

Marketplaces are governed by rules and regulations and as a marketplace administrator our role was to make sure that the best seller won. But that didn't mean that the long tail of sellers wouldn't sell anything. YouTube, for example, has the largest repository of videos. For ShopClues it was important to help buyers discover sellers, but also promote genuine selling.

It was also to do with the Internet, which, by spirit, is an open platform, but it also need checks and balances in place.

At Droom, too, it's not different. But people try to game it. There are all sorts of problems. People list the car, sell it, and then two months later they try and sell the same car again. At Droom my experience with ShopClues helps. We keep on plugging holes. Droom faces its own set of problems where dealers create various ways to make money.

I learnt about some of these problems when I was working with Microsoft. Bill Gates said, 'The good news is people like to use Windows and Office. Bad news is they don't want to pay for it, so there is software piracy. But the worst will be if they stop using Windows and Office.'

I remember Gates saying that it always made him happy that people were using Microsoft's platforms, even if it was in a pirated form. Gates had successfully created a platform that people loved and were even ready to pirate to use it. People used a platform only when they needed something, or there was enough talk around it.

THE ONLINE GOLD RUSH

The boom that happened in Indian courier companies at the time was similar to what happened to the makers of shovels and axes, and the people who owned hotels and eateries during the gold rush in California. They made a lot more money than those who came to find gold. In fact, Indian e-commerce companies made less than three categories of beneficiary companies—Facebook and Google that made money through ads, payment gateway companies that charged their fees and courier companies.

Back in 2011, even though I had spent many years tracking numerous Internet companies—the best of the lot—I was amazed at the pace of change in India.

We had dropped the Northeast from our plans, but the smaller cities in different parts of India had started warming up to the idea of e-commerce. ShopClues was soon doing about 10,000 orders every day. Initially, it was very expensive to deliver. We started at Rs 80 for every packet, but managed to bring it down to Rs 35 in the next six months. It was all about the economics of scale. It was Rs 80 when we were doing roughly 200 orders a day, but came down to Rs 35 once we reached 2,000 orders a day. Thereafter, for months together, we grew 200–300 per cent month-on-month. ShopClues was growing like weed at the time.

Those were the days when e-commerce companies didn't do much except offer big discounts to attract customers. The concept of a healthy unit economics—money made per product sold—had not yet entered the e-commerce business in India. The entire industry has a single-point agenda—to increase gross merchandising value or GMV.

Everyone likes a great deal, so I came up with a plan that was an instant hit. I struck a deal whereby we sold Reebok's aviator sunglasses at a discounted price of Rs 99 against an MRP of Rs 2,500. We sold 1,800 units in one hour! However, there was one deal that burnt a hole in our pocket. In January 2012, our idea was to offer a flat 15 per cent discount on every product but an oversight turned that figure into 50 per cent. Our system generated an email every time someone placed an order on the website. Suddenly, the number of mails had rocketed. By the time I realized the error, we had lost many lakhs in a matter of couple of hours. This also gave me a sense of the success rate of deals. Soon deals became a regular offering on our website.

We wanted deal seekers to shop with us, but we also wanted to grow our base of loyal and happy customers. On Valentine's Day in 2012, we sold 250 flower bouquets but none of them reached their destination due to irresponsible behaviour and wrong commitment by the seller. I felt terrible. To regain trust, we not only refunded the money but we also sent a soft teddy bear and a cake to each of the aggrieved customers.

Putting this fiasco behind us, I came up with two new plans—Jaw-Dropping Deal and Outrageous Deal—to attract more customers. I spent hours with our designer to come up with the logos for both initiatives. Radhika worked as vice president of marketing and I worked very closely with her. She used a lot of American terms and jargons while speaking. The names of the new deals were a deliberate attempt to give American-sounding names to our campaigns. These resonated well with the buyers. We soon launched the Sunday Flea market—again a very American concept—and it became very popular.

We used American names for the campaigns but we were totally Indian when it came to ethos. India is a land dotted with weekly marketplaces that are not only popular but also offer the ease of being able to display a very large number of goods and clothing at the same place. We adopted the concept of a neighbourhood marketplace and it resonated really well with the Indian market. But we didn't want to be identified as a deal site only; hence we quickly cut down on the deals and kept them limited to a couple of days. Unfortunately, like every other e-commerce player, ShopClues also took the easy way out—offering deep discounts and heavy deals. That wasn't the case while I was there.

MOVIES AND STARTUPS

When I started ShopClues there was a clear shortage of talent, especially for e-commerce and Internet marketing. Much like in 1850s California where there was a lot of gold but there were no good houses to live in! At times it was difficult to even find a decent hotel. My startup journey was similar. There was a lot of promise of growth, but there was lack of talent. When I was working in Silicon Valley, the kind of people who worked at startups was much better than in India. Be it an engineer, a finance guy, an HR person or someone handling legal or marketing roles—most of them were talented.

In India variability was huge. That made it very difficult to get talent. What made things more difficult was that there were few startups which had made their name in the market. Anyone wanting to work with a startup headed to those companies. We were left with the bread under the cream in a pastry. Some even thought us to be a fly-by-night operator. Movies like *Social Media* (on Facebook's initial days) and success stories of Flipkart and MakeMyTrip, among others, opened up opportunities for the next generation of startups. With Swiggy and Zomato, there was enough growth happening in the market. But these larger startups with fancier offices attracted most of the talent too.

People referred to the US companies where the startup culture started in the 1950s. When Tom Perkins, who started Kleiner Perkins after completing his MBA programme in Stanford, and two people, Bill Hewlett and David Packard, started HP, Silicon Valley's startup ecosystem was getting ready for its next 70 years of bull run.

That was an advantage. Silicon Valley had 70 years of jumpstart—

the startup culture was deeply engrained in the hearts of technology enthusiasts who wanted to start something on their own.

THE OUTLIER APPROACH

When it came to planning, we always worked backwards. We knew our maximum budget, and we worked on what I call a 'psychological pricing' that would provoke the customer to spend on our platform. We didn't want to celebrate and encourage shoppers only on Diwali, Mother's Day or Valentine's Day—how you performed as a company depended a lot more on how you were seizing your opportunities every single day. To take ourselves to the customers, I calculated how much it would cost us to get a customer through Google, Facebook and other channels. The deal route was cheaper. Even in the first week of our operation, the average cost of acquiring a customer through deals was a third of what it took otherwise.

Looking back, the deodorant deal in June 2012 was a tipping point in ShopClues history. We had reached 25,000 registered users by then. For the next fifty special deals we offered on ShopClues, the popularity was phenomenal. Every time we launched a deal, our website crashed because of customer overload. My analysis of performance-based marketing and our approach of treating customers as kings every day created a very large number of loyal customers for ShopClues.

Sometimes, when I look back, this approach of positive customer stickiness laid our foundation and helped us become a billion dollar company in January 2016. This achievement happened soon after I had relinquished the leadership of the company. Becoming a unicorn wasn't easy. I even created our future income statement and worked hard to achieve the planned goals. As the CEO of the company, I was acutely aware that the 'buck stopped with me'. I personally tracked 4,000 metrics, which included Facebook likes, what percentage of the likes were organic, the traffic mix, mobile vs non-mobile users, customer traffic analysis by region and order analysis by category. All this helped me create strong data analytics and measurement and reporting layers for the company's performance.

There were many ways in which we were operating differently. One key differentiator was my dislike for cash-on-delivery as it was a high-cost model, and there were lots of returns due to delivery issues. We offered ClueBucks and it worked like a miracle. While most of our competitors had 80 per cent of their orders coming from COD, our percentage was just 8 per cent. Even the investors were surprised. They were used to high contribution from COD on the funding decks. Once an investor, who had also invested in another e-commerce company, asked, 'Have you forgotten to add a zero to the COD contribution number?' It worked in our favour.

We were the outliers of the e-commerce world. We were also the first company in the world to offer fulfilment-as-a-service from Day One of our operations. If you look at eBay, the first e-marketplace, they never offered fulfilment service. Amazon, for the first nine years, was not a marketplace. They were only inventory-led companies and provided fulfilment for only those sellers who wanted to avail it. Hence, ShopClues became the first full-stack e-commerce firm in India.

THE MOBILE GENERATION

When ShopClues started, our traffic from mobile phones was almost nothing, but it grew sharply in the next few years. As a result, even though we were the 35th player to enter the Indian e-commerce space, by July 2012 we were the fourth largest. Only Flipkart, Snapdeal and eBay were bigger than us.

Soon we ran out of warehouse space. We were doing close to 4,000 orders every day and the engine had started firing. ShopClues going public was just a matter of time.

It was time to celebrate the successes, so I decided to go take the family for a vacation to the US in July 2013. I had not given up my green card yet. It was the perfect vacation—I took my kids to Disneyland, partied with friends and ate at fancy restaurants—until 29 July.

18

THE DREAM IS SHATTERED

July of 2013 was amazing. With the stress of ShopClues' fledgling days behind me, I vacationed after a long time in the US with my wife and kids. Another high was that our company was definitely on its way to joining India's billion-dollar club in the near future. By this time, I had a strong feeling that we had arrived and it was just a matter of time before we would be listed on Nasdaq, a dream I had nurtured for a long time.Radhika and the kids went to the US on 5 July 2013 and I joined them on 15 July. We met all our old friends and took our kids to show them the house in Fremont Mission Hills, where we had lived until 2011. We also visited Napa Valley, Disneyland, Universal Studios and many other places. It was turning out to be the best trip we had had ever since we moved to India.

On 28 July, we had dinner with Ambrish Srivastava and his wife Dolly at their new swanky home in Menlo Park and many of our other old friends in the US. We decided to spend the night with Rahul Jairath.

I will never forget the minutest details of the days that followed. Rahul made us tea the following morning. After breakfast, Rahul, Radhika and I went to a nearby mall. From there we went to a restaurant for lunch. After shopping and a sumptuous lunch at the Cheesecake Factory in San Jose, we returned to Rahul's place.

As Rahul was parking the car in the garage and I was sitting in the front co-passenger seat, four cars came to a screeching halt—one right beside us and three behind us. I was scared as hell and had no idea who these people were. They were looking for me.

MEETING THE FBI

'This is the FBI,' one of the men shouted. 'Who among you is Sandeep Aggarwal?'

I took a couple of steps forward.

'You have to come with us,' the officer told me, showing me an arrest warrant.

My wife was looking on helplessly, and my kids were confused. Rahul froze.

Even before I could ask the charge, the officer said, 'You have been charged for insider trading.' They turned to my wife and said, 'We will have to take Mr Aggarwal with us.'

I had never been more scared. The vacation had turned into a nightmare within seconds. I was asked to empty my pockets and was bundled into one of their cars. They even asked me to remove the laces of my shoes, lest I strangled one of the officers in the car. I did everything without uttering a single word.

Before leaving, they told Radhika that I was being taken to Contra Costa Detention Center, on the outskirts of San Francisco. While I was leaving I saw tears rolling down my wife's eyes.

IN FBI CUSTODY

The moment I was in the car, the officer sitting beside the driver took out his wireless handset and said, 'He is in our possession.'

Two hours later, at around 5:30 in the evening we reached the Contra Costa prison. 'You'll have to stay here for the night. We'll come in the morning to fetch you,' one of the officers told me. I had no clue what was going on.

I was put inside an overnight prison cell with twenty-five other men who were also to be presented in front of judges the next morning. Shortly thereafter, I was taken for a medical examination. I sat there waiting for my turn, with mostly criminals, drug addicts or men from the mafia. There was one stinking toilet in the holding area but I decided against using it. Most of the people arrested seemed like regulars; they chatted among themselves, boasting about the crimes they had committed. I was afraid, very afraid to be there.

Once the medical examination was over I was given an apple, some juice and a sandwich. By then it was late night and I was ravenous. I called my wife after eating using a collect call phone in the cell. We could barely hear each other, but I figured she was crying inconsolably.

MY LIFE'S OVER

In the morning, some officers picked me up and took me to the FBI headquarters in San Francisco, 30 minutes from the prison centre. At the FBI office, they took my DNA sample, mug shots and noted down some basic information, including my parents' address.

From there, the FBI agents took me to the courthouse where I was put in another holding cell for a few hours until my court hearing was due. Here, the scene was similar to what I had only seen in Hollywood movies—prisoners wearing orange jumpsuits were either roaming around or in the cells, and most of them looked like bona fide criminals. I was in shock and shivering with fear. I was taken to the court of a federal judge. Radhika was already there. She was a complete mess. Thankfully, two of my friends were accompanying her—Rahul Jairath and Nagendra Shukla.

Rahul whispered, 'It's all over the news.' The government agencies wanted to inform the US SEC Securities and Exchange Commission (SEC) and they had already tweeted about my arrest.

Radhika had already spoken to one of our friends, Harmeet Kaur Dhillon, a top attorney and a US-born Indian. Harmeet had sent one of her juniors, probably an intern. I was a little worried seeing someone so young arguing the future course of my life. I was desperate to get out of prison. While the public prosecutors asked the judge to send me to jail, I managed to secure bail, but I knew it would be a dark and long winter.

LONG WALK ON THE BROADWAY

After securing bail in San Francisco, my case was moved to New York City and the same week I had to reappear in front of another judge in Southern District of New York to re-establish my bail. Radhika and I flew to New York. Two of my friends, with whom I had done my MBA—Ayushman Hazarika and Amit Anand—lived in New Jersey and New York City. They stood by my side like pillars. For me, the two of them and their respective spouses, Sonali Hazarika and Ruchika Anand, will remain godsend. These four friends of mine reminded me again and again that in tough times, the most important thing you have are the relationships you have built over the years.

Amit and Ayushman insisted we stay at Amit's condo in Upper West Side in Manhattan. Neither Amit nor Ayushman nor their amazingly gracious wives ever asked if I had really committed a crime. They were friends. They trusted me unconditionaly.

Radhika and I decided to meet a few lawyers. Most of them had already heard about my arrest because I was on the front page of most newspapers and magazines or the home page of online news portals that week. Every lawyer we met told us: 'You seem like a really nice person who was at the wrong place at the wrong time. What Preet Bharara has done to you is called "shock and awe" and it is crafted to create additional pressure on you to agree to their criminal charges and not contest them.' If that had not been their strategy, there would have been no need to arrest me, keep me in a cell overnight and tweet about my arrest.

Most lawyers told me that ever since Preet Bharara had been appointed as the United States Attorney for the most coveted Southern District of New York in 2009, he had made it his mission to crack down on all alleged insider trading cases. He had a nearly 100 per cent conviction rate. Everyone told me the same thing—all the odds are against you. I became even more scared. At the time I had no way of knowing that the legendary Preet Bharara's conviction rate would eventually decline and that he would be forced to drop numerous insider trading cases he had filed between 2009 and 2014.

Preet Bharara was the same United States Attorney who had successfully prosecuted extremely high profile cases including that of Rajat Gupta of McKinsey, Raj Rajaratnam of Galleon and Anil Kumar of McKinsey. He also had two portfolio managers—Todd Newman of Diamondback and Anthony Chiasson of Level Global—convicted for insider trading, but their conviction was later overturned by the appeals court. Bharara was the same person who charged an Indian diplomat in the US, Devyani Khobragade, with visa fraud. A US news anchor called Preet Bharara a 'self-loathing Indian' after he ordered the strip search of Devyani.

That day, Radhika and I spent the entire day meeting many top law firms in the financial district of New York City. The general caution sounded by all the attorneys we met was that it would not be easy to get out of this. First, we would spend a few million dollars to go to a trial, then face the grand jury that was likely to go against anyone from Wall Street due to the suffrage of common people during the mortgage meltdown of 2008. The attorneys also said that if I won the trial, I would get my name cleared, but if I lost, I would lose everything I ever had, including my name, reputation, money and I would also be spending years in prison.

As we were walking on Broadway Street, right in the heart of the financial district of the city, Radhika paused and said, 'Sandeep, I think we are finished.' She was crying.

I decided that I was not going to sink. I started with finding the best lawyer to represent me. Among the many attorneys I met was Sean Casey, who was working with Kobre and Kim. I felt reassured speaking to him and decided to hire him. Sean gave us the details of the firm's legal fee and the payment plan. We did not have the money he asked for. Even the initial payment of $100,000 was out of reach at that point. My wife had already withdrawn $50,000 for my bail and all I had left in the bank was $20,000.

My friends offered to help, but I didn't want to take any financial assistance. It was my battle and I had to fight it on my own. Ambrish Srivastava went out of his way and instead of offering to help, he said, 'You need the money, so take it from me. You can return it later.' His wife Dolly also told me something that I will never forget: 'Sandeep, you are among the nicest people, keep your chin up and we are always there for you.'

FACEBOOK SAVED ME

The legal fee was not the only stress point. ShopClues was still very much in its cash burn phase and we needed more money to sustain the business. The kids' school admission fees were also to be paid soon and my son Ahaan's fee that year was coming to $28,000.

I decided to sell all my stocks. Some of the stocks I held were of Facebook. I had bought them at $17 and now they were trading for roughly $35. Despite knowing that the FB stock would eventually go up to $150, I had no option but to sell everything I had.

Now I had enough money to pay the first instalment to the law firm, and I did it without borrowing a penny from anyone. It was for the first time in 15 years that I had touched my stock trading account. I still have that account but there are no stocks in it. Even though I knew I was in safe hands, I always kept thinking. *What if I am sent back to jail*? On 16 August, Radhika and the kids left for India. I could not leave the US because of my case.

What would happen to ShopClues without me? Because of the time difference between the US and India, I would be on calls and Skype with my wife and the ShopClues team throughout the night. Days were spent reading for my case, researching, talking to my attorney and preparing the defence.

The legal costs kept mounting and it was then that I decided to sell off my real estate assets. I called my friend Vishesh Tandon in Ahmedabad and took his help to sell all my properties—one in Ahmedabad and the rest in Gurgaon and Pune. However, due to softness in the real estate market, we could not see any interest from buyers in a timely manner.

ShopClues, meanwhile, was doing well. The company had reached $20–25 million in gross merchandise value, and was growing at 650 per cent, which was the best any e-commerce company had done. I owned one-third of my company's stocks, but I never wanted to sell any part of it until I had taken ShopClues for an initial public offer. But these were desperate times. I decided to sell 15 per cent of my total holding. I was so desperate that I agreed to sell off the stocks at a price that was 10 months old.

The moment the money came into my account, I transferred a sizeable amount to my wife's account. Now, with money in the bank, I was ready to fight the tough legal battle ahead.

I had reached a point where I had to take several important decisions for the family. It had become increasingly clear that it would be years before I could free myself from the case and return to India, hence I had sent Radhika and the kids back home. The three reasons for this were: 1) continuity, stability and normalcy for the kids so that their emotional state and education would not suffer; 2) continuity for our household so that things became less harsh for Radhika; and 3) if Radhika was close to ShopClues, we would decrease the chances of the company going belly up. I must say that sending them back to India was among the hardest things I have ever done in my life. Rahul stood by me and so did Amit and Ayushman, but life was going from hard to very hard.

I stayed with Rahul Jairath after returning from New York to San Jose, where I lived until February 2014. During the time I stayed with Rahul, he was my father, my mother and my best friend.

THE CHARGES CHANGE ME

In the three months after I was first charged, I started feeling significant changes in me. Not in any order, but I started avoiding meeting friends, colleagues and acquaintances. My confidence got eroded significantly. At night I was not able to sleep and even if I managed a wink, I never had any dreams whatsoever. I had always been a workaholic but now I started working even more and even tried to battle the constraints imposed by time. I became adept at juggling many things—my legal case, ShopClues, kids, wife and parents. I also became more and more spiritual. I do not think I would have survived that phase of my life without my spiritual progress. My elder sister Reeta and her husband Rajiv Gupta lived in Silicon Valley and they started taking me to a Shiva temple in Sunnyvale. Apart from signing up as a volunteer at the temple, I learnt many mantras and also started meditating. I tried to do as much seva as I could at the temple. One day that stands out in my memory is the day Mahashivratri was celebrated. That day I felt a sense of energy running through me and it gave me the strength to live through the dark times and eventually find peace and solace.

Among the friends who were there for me unconditionally and who always went the extra mile to make me feel comfortable and whom I could not ever think of avoiding were Ram Menon and his wife Geeta Menon. Radhika and I were very close to Ram and Geeta. Their son is one year older than my elder son Ahaan. Our families spent almost every weekend together before we moved to India.

Two other couples, Sunil and Regina Gupta and Mahesh and Prerana Balakrishnan, also offered every possible help they could. Sunil told Rahul, 'I know Sandeep is avoiding meeting people but we are his friends and really care about him. Whenever he is ready, Regina and I would love to see him.' Sooner rather than later, I did go to their house for dinner.

All this unconditional love and support also resulted in another deep change in me—it instilled a strong sense of gratitude and positivity within me. I looked at every new day as an opportunity to come out of the state of self-pity and self-loathing.

THE EAST RIVER AT MANHATTAN

In the first week of September, I had to decide the future course of action in my legal case. I spent hours with Sean Casey, my attorney. I was staying at Amit's condo in Upper East Side in Manhattan at the time. One day, I was walking down the East River in Manhattan, which was three streets from Amit's condo, while talking to Radhika. During our conversation, I suddenly started crying profusely. She told me to go back to Amit's house right away. Now I think she was worried I might commit suicide by jumping into the river. She called me again in 20 minutes to check if I was back at Amit's house. As I learned later, my friends Ayushman, Amit, Sonali, Ruchika, my parents, my siblings and Rahul, too, had thought I would kill myself. Radhika immediately boarded United's non-stop flight from New Delhi to Newark International Airport in Newark, New Jersey. Next day, Radhika, landed in the US. She took the bus to save $80, which was the taxi fare. When she finally arrived, we cried and cried and finally melted into each other's arms. For the next twenty-five days, Radhika stayed with me.

Around the same time Ayushman told me a story. Amit was also there when this happened. Ayushman said there was a man who was married to a beautiful and loving woman and had three adorable kids. Due to some reason, the man became disabled and his family had to do a lot for him so that he could carry out his daily activities. He thought to himself that if he was no more, his family would be spared the trouble of looking after him and could have a far better life. He decided to jump out of the window of his highrise apartment. Miraculously, he somehow survived but ended up in a much worse condition with full body paralysis. His family again did everything under the sun for his revival and recovery. That's when he realized that he had clearly underestimated what he meant to his family. Ayushman's message was loud and clear and he also made me promise that no matter what, I would keep fighting and not do anything stupid. Ayushman is among the most intense, compassionate and profoundly intuitive persons I have ever met.

I asked him why he was still standing by my side. He said, 'I am selfish and I want the Sandeep of old back. I again want the great friend who was funny, caring and loving. So now you know, all this is because I am selfish.' I had tears in my eyes and so did Ayushman and Amit. This pep talk gave me the much-needed hope and the strength to keep moving forward, again.

PLEADING GUILTY

The charges against me had their genesis in something that had happened on 9 July 2009 during the time I was working as a senior Internet research analyst at Collins Stewart.

The allegations were that I received non-public information that day from a contact at Microsoft, who told me of a possible Search partnership between Microsoft and Yahoo. At the time, news of this possible partnership had already been doing the rounds after an unsuccessful attempt by Microsoft to acquire Yahoo in a deal valued over $40 billion in 2007. However, according to the authorities, I had received 'specific' material and non-public information, and passed it on to Richard Lee, a portfolio manager at the now infamous hedge fund, SAC Capital (named after Steven A. Cohen, a billionaire and among the 50 richest people globally). Lee bought Yahoo stock at the prevailing prices and sold them at a higher price when the deal was announced.

Lee pleaded guilty and agreed to testify for the government three days before I was charged. I soon realized that the investigation's main target was SAC. The government agencies had been chasing the hedge fund for over a decade but could not act because of lack of evidence. They evidently believed that I would be able to help them take down SAC.

I knew my case would make things difficult at ShopClues. So I decided to step down from the position of CEO on 13 October 2013, and recommended to the board that Sanjay replace me as the CEO. I could have made my wife the CEO, but I wasn't sure if we would be living in India for long. Things were different then. I trusted Sanjay and was confident that he, along with Radhika and me, would work as a team and ensure prosperity for the company.

On 8 November 2013, seven days after my dad's 71st birthday and one day after Ahaan's 10th, I pleaded guilty based upon my understanding of what the US insider-trading law was at that time (an understanding that would later prove to be erroneous), and took full responsibility for my conduct in the insider-trading case, signed up as a cooperating witness and entered a plea bargaining agreement with the government. What followed were a series of meetings with the Justice Department, the FBI and the Securities and Exchange Commission as part of my cooperation agreement.

Towards the end of November, I wanted to visit India. It was my parents' 50th wedding anniversary on 6 December. I made a request to the US government to allow me to visit India. The approval came through on 4 December, and I took the first available flight to India. I was with my family on the evening of 6 December. For the past two years my sister and I had planned this day. But with me going through a crisis, we decided on a low-key affair. It was an extremely emotional moment for everyone, especially me. Everyone had tears in their eyes. I was in India after five months and had never been so happy to be back.

SHOPCLUES IN TROUBLE

Next day, my wife decided to surprise everyone at ShopClues and invited them home without telling anyone that I was back. I opened the door every time someone came. Some of them screamed in delight on seeing me, some lifted me up in their arms and some started crying. I was overwhelmed and felt blessed for the relationships I had built.

ShopClues was not in the best of shape, though. From a 650 per cent growth in July when I had gone to the US, it had fallen under 100 per cent. The fall was not because ShopClues had become too big to continue growing at that pace.

When I stepped into the office the next day, it felt as if it was an old-style laidback office. The energy levels of the people were down. The walls, corridors and hallways, which once adorned pictures of achievers and go-getters, were bare. I decided it was time to rise again. I gathered the team to understand the issues that had slowed us and discussed the possible solutions. Within hours, I was ready with our next moves.

I had three priorities: boost the morale of the employees, get the company back on a high-growth path and raise the next round of capital.

19

THE PARTING

The year 2013 was big for the e-commerce business in India. Flipkart, the leader of the pack, had raised $360 million in new funding, while Snapdeal raised $125 million. This was also the time when Jeff Bezos was revving the Amazon juggernaut to crash into the e-commerce market in India. I had to act decisively, otherwise ShopClues could easily turn into a nightmare. The signs of ShopClues slowly losing the plot were quite visible. In fact, one of our investors, Teruhide Sato, was among the first to point this out on a visit to the ShopClues office in December 2013. Teru, short for Teruhide Sato, was the founder of Beenext, a venture capital firm.

'What's not right, Teru?' I asked him.

He sipped his coffee, looked at me, paused for a few seconds and said, 'ShopClues appears old and lethargic. The energy of a startup isn't there.' Many years later, Teru told me, 'Sandeep, I invest in people and the energy of the company is a key determinant of deciding to invest. I want to see people who are excited about what they are building.' He was spot on—the energy and vibrancy had gone missing from ShopClues during the time I was in the US.

Before the entire US episode, we had celebrated every small and big achievement—from a corporate award to meeting daily and weekly targets, or even small spikes of traffic that came our way because of the experiments we tried. All that had changed. Now, the list of problems seemed never ending. Even the money we had would last us not more than four to five months. No investor was ready to bet on ShopClues. It was time to redefine ShopClues.

AN OUTSIDER IN MY OWN BACKYARD

The only way to survive was to get more funds, but how? In a market where there were bigger and more famous e-commerce companies, we had to communicate our differentiation to potential investors. I knew that if we could demonstrate that, money would start pouring in. The company was still growing fast, but not at the rate that would excite new investments. It was important that I took back the reigns of the company. However, some of the existing investors didn't want me back. They wanted ShopClues' single largest shareholder—me—to exit.

There was no way I would part with ShopClues. It was nothing less than a child to me. As the founder I knew that ShopClues was weak and vulnerable. I started spending a lot of time in the office tracking every move of our competitors. But some of the investors made it clear that I wasn't welcome in my own company anymore. Another investor even called to say I should stop coming to the office because potential investors might get the wrong message. At the time, the company was already in talks for more funds. Sanjay Sethi was the CEO by now. He was supposed to handle the show—the show I had created from scratch.

Things started unravelling rapidly. At an annual party organized by an investor, all the team members were invited except me. Soon we hosted that investor at our office. The meeting went on for three hours, but the investor didn't look at me even once. It was clear that he didn't want me there. However, I deep down, I still knew that ShopClues was still dependent on me.

My legal case did not shatter me as much as knowing that my investors wanted to get rid of me. Radhika was as broken as me. While I resigned as CEO of ShopClues in October 2013, I realized in January 2014 that I was no longer welcome at ShopClues by the large existing investors.

MEETING DEEP KALRA, AGAIN

Before my legal case, I had never even had a single traffic ticket, let alone a charge as serious as the insider trading charges I had been accused of. What really bothered me was, *How did I end up in this mess*? I had no clear answers to this question. Had I done anything that my conscience would not allow? Despite my plea of admitting guilt to the charges based on a misunderstanding of the insider trading law (by myself, my lawyers, and even the prosecutors and the judge) I did not truly feel that my conduct in the case had gone against my conscience.

Through thick and thin, my friends and family never abandoned me. Most of them never made me feel that I had been accused of financial fraud. But there were also others, mostly from the financial world, who had convicted me already. I decided to limit my interactions with them.

When I was back in India, one day I called Deep Kalra, expecting nothing more than just a cordial chat. I was in for a surprise—he invited me over to discuss business.

This was going to be my first full-fledged professional meeting after my legal case. The meeting happened at MakeMyTrip's head office in Gurgaon. Deep's old friend and co-founder of MakeMyTrip, Rajesh Magow, joined us.

I was extremely nervous, but to my relief there was not even an iota of condescension from them. I ended up asking Deep, 'Why are you being so nice to me?'

Deep laughed and said, 'Sandeep, one day when you are out of this [legal case] and write your memoir, I want to be a part of it.' A vote of confidence from someone of Deep's stature was a rare occurrence in my life. It was an incredibly emotional moment for me, and even till this day I remember every bit of it vividly. It meant the world to me. For me MakeMyTrip was always a very special company because its Nasdaq listing and meeting Deep had served as triggers for me to become an entrepreneur.

That meeting with Deep made me believe in my entrepreneurial abilities again. My dream of building an Internet company out of India was reinforced. I felt happy again.

Over the years I have learnt a lot from Deep. In fact, it was during this phase that I started reading a lot of books, especially autobiographies of famous leaders and business tycoons. Reading them helped me a lot in forming my understanding and opinion.

Even as an analyst, whenever I met any of the founders of large companies, like Larry Page, Sergey Brin or Bill Gates, I would observe their behaviour, body language and how they would articulate their viewpoints to get a sense of how they ran and managed their companies. Deep is one such technology entrepreneur from India, a rarity in 2010. Sanjeev Bikhchandani of Naukri.com was the other one. Both of them paved the way for other Indian Internet companies.

In those days, perhaps I was looking for some validation and I ended up calling many other acquaintances from the industry, just to gauge their views towards my legal case.

It would not be an exaggeration to say there were times when I felt that I did not have any grip over my life or career and went around like a headless chicken. Soon it was time for me to go back to the US.

RETURN TO THE US

My cooperation with the US government made it necessary for me to go back to the US in January 2014. However, no matter what, ShopClues was still my responsibility. I kept planning the next moves for the company and developing more business ideas in a laser-focused manner.

13 March 2014. I was staying with my sister in Silicon Valley. That day I woke up and had an epiphany: 'The worst thing a human being can do is have self-pity.' I had to move on. The writing had been on the wall for a while but I had refused to accept it. I finally made up my mind to move on from ShopClues after the next round

of funding. I told Radhika about the decision. She also knew how deeply connected I was with the company, but she also knew that the investors wanted me out. Accepting reality was very difficult for both of us. She cared deeply about me and suggested I get involved with something else and forget ShopClues.

I made up my mind to plan my next moves and not waste any time, as I had to stay put in the US without full clarity on when I could go back to India. I was missing my family unimaginably, especially my kids. To feel better, I decided to rent an apartment that was in close proximity to Fremont, California, the place where my family and I had lived for ten years.

I was about to sign the rent lease for the apartment when Anil Advani, the attorney who had incorporated ShopClues for me and had handled all the rounds of raising capital for ShopClues, called me. He also lived in Fremont. When he came to know of my plans to rent an apartment, he offered that I should live with him. At the time he was separated from his wife, and his daughter Khushi visited him once a week. I was very hesitant but I decided to take up his offer. I was very lucky that he was also there for me unconditionally.

BEGINNING, AGAIN

I knew my life with ShopClues was over. I needed to rebuild myself and the only way to do that was build another company. I knew three things very clearly. First, I wanted to be an entrepreneur yet again; second, I had to be in the consumer Internet vertical and third, the business should serve an Indian need to begin with but eventually go global. I always believed there was going to be long-term growth and large-scale adoption of digital economy in India. The reason for this assessment was the low penetration of the Internet at that time and the high capital cost in the physical retail sector and the structural problems associated with it.

I knew the smartphone revolution was around the corner. The power of the Internet was about to be unleashed and the common man would drive this transformation.

There was enough opportunity in the space of online payments, another possibility was to create a Yelp-like review website, then there was also space for niche verticals in the e-commerce space, or I could venture into ad-tech products. But I knew there wasn't any space for yet another ShopClues. In the next few days I came up with fifty-two business ideas. It was a difficult choice to make. I screened each idea and the capital that would be needed. Soon my list was down to eight ideas and these ideas were those that could be executed while being in the US. On further analysis, I was down to two options—an online mobile wallet or something in the automobile space.

EARLY TO THE PARTY

By the time I started ShopClues, others had already jumped into the e-commerce game. We could never overcome the late-to-the-party phase. By the time ShopClues had become sizeable, Flipkart was already quite ahead, and even Amazon, despite being a late entrant, had become mammoth on the strength of its deep, deep pockets.

In the payments business, Paytm and MobiKwik were already entrenched. I was late and would have to play a chasing game. And in the chasing mode you are more defensive than offensive in your approach. This was one of my biggest learnings from ShopClues. We were the 35th entrants into Indian e-commerce to begin with and within the first eight months we became the fourth largest. But even six years later, our rank hadn't changed. We kept chasing the leaders and they kept growing much more than us on the strength of attracting more funds due to their ranking.

If I had thought of ShopClues a year earlier, I could have perhaps become among the top two in the market. The key is to start early, but not too early. It's vital to time the market by analysing demand and supply. Essentially, if ShopClues had started four to five years before it actually did, it would have shut shop by now. Using actual examples, I did not want to be like MySpace or Orkut. I wanted to be like Facebook. When Facebook was already a name, others jumped in and built social media companies. Some of them even became successful in the short term but ran out of steam eventually. Facebook, on the other hand, was slow to expand but had robust technological support to power their growth.

Being defensive makes a company less innovative. Even though ShopClues was the world's first true marketplace, the company was never part of the market evolution. It had no choice but to go after the existing customers of Flipkart or Snapdeal. The only way to grow was to burn more money than the incumbents.

I also knew that by being in the chasing game and remaining defensive I would never be able to create a world-class company.

The last box that needed to be ticked was that the company had to be an 'in and out' technology company within the digital economy, something like Google's search engine. ShopClues as a marketplace was 50 per cent technology, 25 per cent selling and 25 per cent operations. This time around I was very sure that I did not want operations to be a part of the business. So no picking up an item, then packing and delivering it.

In hindsight, if ShopClues did not have fulfilment as a service, I think it could have become much bigger. Operation-related businesses have a longer gestation period and it results in slow growth. A prime example of this is that Amazon, even after all these years of its existence, is still trying to solve the logistics conundrum.

Also, I was looking at businesses where the gross margins could be in the range of 75–80 per cent, which is impossible in the e-commerce business. That is why my new venture had to be a company that catered to the online automobile customers. It was time to create Droom, an Internet company that would be for the world.

20

AUTOMOBILE ON MOBILE

Droom was born as a mobile-first company, which means that the platform was designed to suit the small handhelds. So much so that in its first year Droom did not even have a website. The mobile boom had already started by the time I launched Droom. Smartphones had started replacing computers as the primary device to access the Internet. It was important for me as an entrepreneur to build a company around the primary customer, and the desktop versions would follow.Apart from the technology, the organizational and legal structures were all aligned for Droom to become a global company. I can happily say that Droom has become a global company.

BILL GATES, THE VISIONARY

Many of the plans I had for Droom were things I learnt at Microsoft, especially from Bill Gates. His vision was phenomenal. He focused on three things: always chase big and yet addressable opportunities, keep your focus on high gross margin and always do something where technology plays the central role. Except high gross margins, I had implemented the other two things at ShopClues.

There was one more key learning from my days as an analyst on Wall Street that I started believing in more and more when I turned entrepreneur—it's better to be lucky than smart. That said, luck is also about preparing yourself to be at the right place at the right time and seize the opportunity. I continue to believe in luck, which includes lucky dates. I started ShopClues on 21 November 2011, and then I decided the launch Droom on 21 November 2014. I also started Droom from the same office where we started ShopClues.

A NEW APPROACH

Many entrepreneurs carry too much baggage from their past and it tends to weigh them down always. While I learnt a lot from ShopClues, it was important to shed the burden of its legacy and start afresh. Droom deserved a new approach. It would have been criminal to use the ShopClues templates at Droom. For me the experience was about falling in love with the new company like it's a new love in my life. That was the passion with which I decided that Droom was going to be my new business. That day was 14

April 2014, the first day of the Hindu calendar.

The next day, I called my wife and told her, 'I know what I am doing next—Droom.' She sounded very puzzled about its meaning. I simply said, 'The revving up of a car's engine is represented by the word, vroom. Instead, I will call the new company Droom. The 'D' comes from the word dream, which is what buying a car is for most people.' 'Vroom' and 'dream' combined to become Droom. Also, Droom sounded youthful, energetic and vibrant. For the first time, it seemed that everything was coming together yet again. Radhika endorsed my suggestion and I couldn't have been happier for having chosen that name. Later, I also came to know that droom means dream in Dutch.

From then till May I was literally glued to my seat, working almost seventeen hours a day. The remaining time got divided between a few hours of sleep, playing golf or hitting the gym.

In those weeks I built 127 screens, which was the wireframe for the Droom application. I created the entire product vision, page by page. I knew how Droom would look in its first phase.

RAISING FUNDS

My confidence in my ability to attract investors was low, mainly because of two reasons: my on-going legal case and the fact that I had to resign from ShopClues. These reasons were actually interconnected. I kept thinking: 'Why in hell would someone give me money for any new business?'

Nonetheless, I decided not to die wondering.

Teru Sato, an investor in ShopClues, and I had stayed in touch, even during my worst times. I requested Teru for an appointment.

Till that point, apart from my wife, I had not spoken to anyone about Droom. In my mind I was still married to ShopClues. Making Droom succeed was the only way to bury the past. One day Teru called me and said, 'Sandeep, I am going to be in San Francisco next week.'

We met at a fancy restaurant in Chinatown. I showed Teru the wireframes I had made. He was immediately interested. We were there for the next 4–5 hours and gulped down many pints of beer. Before we knew it, it was time for the place to close. Our meeting was far from over. We decided to move the meeting to Holiday Inn, which had a bar that remained open till 2 a.m. Teru and I spent the next few hours talking more about Droom and gulping down even more beer.

Finally it was time to ask for the money. 'Teru, I need $350,000 initially, and I have a commitment for $200,000, so I am looking for $150,000 from you,' I told him hesitantly.

'Sandeep, I can't give you $150,000,' Teru said with a straight face. I was heartbroken. I thought of the time when I had applied for internship while pursuing MBA in the US. Almost every company I had met had turned me down. 'Sandeep, we really enjoyed meeting you. You are very energetic and intelligent, however ...'

Teru looked at me and started smiling. Was he happy at my misery? He suddenly had a glow in his eyes and stretched out his arm for a handshake and said, 'I can't give you $150,000; I want to deploy a minimum of half a million dollars.'

I was on the verge of tears. It's impossible to describe the feeling that overcame me. Months of despondency and desperation had suddenly faded away.

Teru said he would go back to Japan and get back with the final contours of the deal after discussing with his company's board members. I also decided to approach Chaim Friedman and Itschak Friedman, who were the first angel investors at ShopClues, in case Teru's company changed their mind. I told them about my idea. They heard me for 45 minutes over a Skype call and asked for time to get back to me. The presentation to the Friedmans was so much similar to the time I had approached them to raise funds for ShopClues. They called back within hours and said, 'Count us in for $200,000.'

Suddenly, from being scared about raising money, I was looking forward to launching the company. A day after the Friedmans committed their share, Teru also called from Japan. He said, 'Sandeep, you know we are a public company, there are board members, and there are many members. So I had to discuss with everyone. They all loved the idea and now we are wondering if you would accept one million dollars.'

As someone who had spent almost a decade on Wall Street analysing Internet companies, I knew what it meant to have an investor raising its commitment twice—from $150,000 to $500,000, and then to $1,000,000.

I knew Teru was fond of me and despite my legal troubles and moving out from ShopClues, he believed in my entrepreneurial skills. I knew it was a done deal.

I did not need any more money at that point but I still called the Friedmans. I told them that Teru had decided to put in a million. He thought I would decline their offer of $200,000, but I took it. It was entirely because of the trust the Friedmans had in me. They wanted to invest in my venture for a second time. Now they wanted to bump up their amount as well. 'Can you make it a quarter of a million?' Chaim said. I agreed immediately. With $1.25 million in my kitty in June of 2014, I was ready to take Droom off the ground.

There was good news from India too—ShopClues had successfully raised its Series C funding.

SEEDING EARLY FOR A FUTURE VC ROUND

One critical aspect of entrepreneurship that I can swear by is the importance of relationships. Most of the key team members as well as investors that I ended up working with at both ShopClues and Droom were due to the relationships I had built over the years.

Sid Talwar, who is a partner at Lightbox and, since 2015, has also been a board member at Droom, is a prime example of how relationships matter more than anything else. I was introduced to Sid, shortly after I had moved to India in 2011, by his partner and childhood friend, Sandeep Murthy, who ran Kleiner Perkins and Sherpalo for India. In August 2011, when I had raised $1.95 million in the angel round for ShopClues, Sandeep Murthy and his friends Jeremey Wenokur, Sunny Rao and Shiv Puri had invested in ShopClues. And when I was raising the Series A funding for ShopClues in January 2012, Sid Talwar also decided to invest in ShopClues in his personal capacity. Sid has been a friend and advisor ever since.

A week after I told Radhika about Droom, Sid called to ask how I was. When I told him about Droom and its fund-raising plans, he sounded enthusiastic and I explained my idea to him. By that time, Teru Sato and Friedman had already confirmed their investments in Droom. Sid was then in the midst of launching an India-focused VC fund along with three other partners whom I have known for many years. Due to his preoccupation, the discussions with Sid did not progress.

After I raised another round for Droom in October 2014 (Series 2), Sid expressed his desire to spend time with me to understand Droom and our plans. I made a trip to Mumbai in November 2014 to meet Sid. He also made me meet Rishab Malik, who joined Droom in January 2015 as the head of business development. Even though we already had more than twenty employees by then, I decided to give Rishab co-founder status. At the time, and even in hindsight, I felt that was a very good decision. An intelligent, committed, dedicated, sincere and senior team member like Rishab can make a huge difference in the journey to build a large and scalable company.

The discussion between Lightbox and Droom continued and finally Lightbox led Series A for Droom and invested close to $10 million in May 2015, one of the largest Series A investments in India at the time.

SETTING UP THE STRUCTURE

I commissioned a designer from Pakistan to design a logo. I also started looking for other consultants to help me with the design.

Droom was going to be an India-focused company, but with a global vision. After establishing ourselves in India, the plan was to expand outside India, starting with Southeast Asia. I had to think of a legal structure that would help me take the business international. I decided to create a Singapore holding company. I had a selfish motive in doing this—the possibility that Singapore could become home for me and my family.

I spoke to my wife about the Singapore idea. The kids' summer break was about to start. We decided she would travel to Singapore with them and complete the formalities of incorporating Droom as a company. Because of my legal case, our financial resources had been stretched to the limit. It was time to sell some more ShopClues shares to remain afloat.

To ensure that the kids had a great time, I booked their stay at a hotel on Sentosa Island. However, Radhika did not like the hotel, so I changed their booking to a hotel in downtown Singapore. Regardless of the change of hotel, the kids were enjoying the vacation and that made me very happy. Our 17th wedding anniversary was only a few days away too.

While sitting in the US, I managed to set up all her meetings with the lawyers and the bank. Radhika opened a bank account on behalf of the company. In Singapore, a foreigner can create a company online but you cannot have a bank account until you visit the bank physically. A lawyer helped us incorporate the company. Back in the US, I was busy building the structure, signing the term sheet, closing documents, opening bank accounts and finding people to hire.

Once the company was incorporated, I closed the first round of funding and money came in the bank. After a long time, exciting things were finally happening around me. My kite was again catching favourable winds and was ready to soar. There was light after months of darkness. I recalled the struggle of the last ten months and the number of times I had wanted to give up. When I look back, I just don't know how I survived those painful days. There were two main factors that motivated me and made me stronger mentally. First: I wanted everyone to respect me once again. Second: There was the desire to provide a good life to my wife and children once again.

HIRING BEGINS

As soon I had received commitments from Teru and the Friedmans, I started hunting for team members. Because of all the negative publicity I had received due to my legal case, I wasn't sure how many people would agree to work with me. Regardless, I started talking to people I knew within the Internet industry. A friend with whom I played squash helped me with one of our first hires. This friend's startup was closing down, so he recommended his vice president of engineering, Mayank Chaudhary, to me. Mayank had completed masters in artificial intelligence from Stanford University and he immediately expressed his willingness to join me.

He became our first vice president of engineering. He quit when I decided to move the operations to India. Though he wasn't around for long, his joining was a big boost to my own confidence and proved that talented people from the industry still wanted to work with me.

21

STARTUP FROM SILICON VALLEY

It was summer in San Francisco. Mark Twain had famously remarked, 'The coldest winter I ever saw was the summer I spent in San Francisco.' That summer was exactly that—it was extremely tough on me. Since my financial position had been compromised due to the ongoing case, I was forced to stay at a cheap motel in San Francisco and paid an average of $70 per night. I was hesitant of sharing this as well as embarrassed, and never disclosed this fact to anyone. Everyone thought I was staying with a friend in Fremont, but I had been staying at the motel Extended Stay America since April. The room was so tiny and basic that during video calls with the family I would often dim the lights, so they could not figure where I was staying. While the place served its purpose and helped me save money, the hygiene levels eventually got to me. I developed a very bad skin allergy that took more than a year to cure.

My food came from an Indian restaurant, Lucky Sweets, owned by a Punjabi family from Jalandhar. My food budget was $10 per day. From owning the latest Mercedes during my analyst days, I was now driving a leased Toyota Prius. There were nights when I would cry and cry. The circumstances were such that even the toughest people would have found it difficult. However, I accepted everything as part of my karma and decided that hard work was the only way to alleviate my suffering.

Regardless of the hardships, I look back at those days with nostalgia because that was the time when the idea of Droom took wings.

A TECHNOLOGY COMPANY

Droom has been fortunate—we had investors who believed in us and people who were passionate. We had money in the bank on the basis of nothing but a basic presentation of my plans. This was in sharp contrast to ShopClues, where funding was scarce.

I had decided early on that Droom would be technology-centric. Hence I wanted to hire people who were on top of the game in the technology business. The proof of the level of importance I gave to technology was when I hired Mayank Chaudhary as vice president (engineering). I not only made him the co-founder of Droom, but his shareholding in the company was also a high single-digit number.

A week after Mayank joined the company, he brought a friend to the office. He was from the Philippines and much older than both of us. 'I would like you to meet Luis De Guzman,' said Mayank. Luis was a terrific programmer who had worked with eBay, Apple and many other large technology companies. We had to hit the ground fast, so I quickly decided to get Luis on board. I asked Mayank to propose a salary and offer Luis some stocks in the company. Luis was keen to work with us and agreed to our offer.

Droom was planned as a marketplace for everything related to cars and bikes—from services like insurance to selling used cars to predicting prices of vehicles based on processes and algorithms. I spent a lot of time with Mayank and Luis planning the three main issues: listing management platform, order management platform and seller management platform. Their job was to create these technology platforms. Meanwhile, I started spending more time in designing the brand's identity, like the Droom logo, company branded merchandising and more.

Droom made me feel that I was finally running a pure startup—something that I had never experienced before. We had cash and a three-member team. All we needed now was an office in Silicon Valley.

DROOMING IN ON THE FIRST OFFICE

One of my friends, Nagendra Shukla, was running ClassHubz, a social networking company for parents in Fremont, very close to the Tesla factory. Nagendra worked from an office that belonged to Manmeet Bhasin, who was running his own company, Dataguise, an IT services firm, from the same premises. Incidentally, Dataguise was the first company where, way back in 2008, I had put in my first angel investment money.

Manmeet agreed to rent out an unused part of his office to Droom. Since the facilities and utilities were common, the overheads were less. The concept of co-working spaces was not very popular then. WeWork wasn't a global phenomenon yet.

BACK IN INDIA

My legal situation slowly started getting better and I even started thinking of a possible acquittal shortly. On 23 May 2014, a meeting was called by the government, in which one of the officers told my attorney, 'Whatever help Sandeep needed to provide us in this case has been done already.' With the burden of the legal case easing up, it was time to take care of my health. Within the next few months I shed twelve kilos.

The basic technology-related work needed for Droom was now in place, thanks to Mayank and Luis. I then decided to shift the operations from the US to India. On 5 August 2014, I took the flight back to India. Before leaving the US, I called up Manoj Sharma, the man who had rented out ShopClues's first office space to me. By then ShopClues had shifted to a fancy address.

Manoj agreed to sublet the basement and the ground floor to me. When I reached India and visited the office, I saw it in a pretty bad state. I hired the same person who had done the interiors for ShopClues.

One of the biggest obstacles I faced upon my return was my past. In the US, most of the people I met did not judge me harshly. They accepted me as a human being. And like every person, I also have flaws. However, my flaws have no bearing on my skills as an entrepreneur. This fact was endorsed when I was able to raise funds for Droom during the time my case was still on. Not just that, the US government allowed me to return to India.

Back in India, things were vastly different. One day a friend who lived in the same apartment complex as me recommended I meet three IIM graduates and see if they were suited for Droom. In all the three meetings, the main point of discussion was my legal case. It was hardly a surprise that none of them decided to join Droom. There were also occasions when even though people knew I was listening, I heard some of them say, 'Oh! This is the guy who was charged for insider trading.' I became extremely cautious and insecure when I was in public. I thought people were judging me and talking about me. Perhaps some innocent comments made by them also got exaggerated in my head.

These experiences made me wonder if Droom would ever attract the kind of talent that was needed to grow. However, I did not allow these irritants deter me and I kept hunting for capable people.

SEPARATE WAYS

Every morning Radhika would leave for ShopClues, the company that I created. By then, ShopClues had reached its peak on the back of the exponential boom in Internet connectivity as well as smartphones. It had created a niche for itself as an online flea market, while companies like Amazon, Flipkart and Snapdeal were selling brands. I felt I also deserved some of the credit for ShopClues' success. Not just that, I was unhappy that I lost out on the monetary benefits because I had been forced to sell my shares in ShopClues. Someone else had plucked the flowers from the rose plant I planted. This issue was eating me up. Often I thought of the possibility of someone snatching Droom from me. I did not speak about these thoughts to anyone, not even Radhika.

I realized the bitter experience at ShopClues had turned me into someone I did not want to be—jealous, bitter and insecure. I decided it was time to change.

MY FIRST INDIA HIRE

One day, Vishal Sharma, the last senior person I hired before my legal trouble started in the US, called me and recommended his former colleague Babita to head Droom's human resource division. Vishal and Babita had worked together at Indiamart. I met her in Gurgaon and within half an hour, I made her an offer. Babita joined as Droom's first India employee.

Soon we were joined by Hiramani Sharma, who had worked with me in ShopClues' cataloguing team. Sumit Vijay, who was product manager at ShopClues, followed him.

Pyush Kumar, who helped me understand technology when I started ShopClues (but could not join us), quit MakeMyTrip and came on board. Pyush got two more people for technology because we needed good engineering resources to build the product.

By now the office was ready and the team had increased to nine. We moved into the new office and Droom was ready to take off.

Finally, Radhika and I were on separate journeys.

22

DROOM, DROOM, DROOM...

As the smartphone revolution swept across India, we decided that Droom would be a mobile-first company. Essentially it means that the platform and the technology that would power the company would primarily cater to people who used their phones as the primary device to access the Internet.

We hired a company called Lets-Go-Mo to build our mobile application. Lets-Go-Mo, which was later acquired by Snapdeal, was an IT services company that built mobile apps. Four people from their team operated from our office and interacted closely with Droomers (employees of Droom). Given the importance of design in the overall scheme of things, I hired two people to work with the four designers from Lets-Go-Mo and called this setup 'Droom Design Studio'.

From my experience of building ShopClues, I knew you need the right talent for every stage of building a next-generation company. By now the team had grown significantly and we were on our way to becoming India's only mobile-first business. Desktop-first was monolithic in comparison to what we were out to achieve. Our focus on mobile phones was to make ourselves much more modular, flexible, nimble-footed and service-oriented.

I was working up to sixteen hours a day but I felt more energetic than ever.

WORN-OUT COMPETITION

After coming back to India and making an even more detailed analysis of the competition that existed for Droom, I soon realized that even though there were other players like CarDekho, CarWale, CarTrade, Quikr, OLX, etc., the consumer experience being offered by Droom was miles ahead. We had what it took to not only create a large customer base on our own but also to wean away users who were on other platforms. The opportunity that Droom had in the automobile market was much bigger than what I ever estimated.

The existing online market was very fragmented and you could not distinguish one site from another. None of these companies were even thinking of the market I wanted to create and cater to.

It was October 2014 when I went back to my investors and told them about this opportunity. I asked them for more capital.

ROUND TWO

I think it was a Sunday when I got a call from Viren Rana, a friend from the US. He had seen the way I had built ShopClues and had heard about my new venture. I told him more about Droom.

'Sandeep, are you planning to raise more capital for Droom?' he asked.

'Yes, I am trying, Viren. I have already spoken to my investors for another round of funding,' I told him.

'Can I invest half a million dollars?' he asked. He was visiting Delhi and we decided to meet for lunch the same day. By the end of lunch, he doubled his commitment to a million!

Within days, Teru had committed another million. Since I did not want to dilute my equity in the company beyond a point, I decided to close this round of funding at three million dollars. So I needed another million. That's when Vishesh Tandon called. He had some affluent friends in Ahmedabad—mostly Patels—who wanted to put in a million dollars into Droom. We were ready to close round two when Chaim Friedman expressed his desire to invest more. So we ended up raising $3.6 million.

BAJAJ PULSAR @ RS 9,999

On 21 November 7:30 p.m. we launched our app on Google Play Store. It was time for the Droomers to celebrate. The party continued till 3:30 a.m.

The days that followed were disappointing. We did not make a single sale till 7 January 2015. I decided to fall back on the tried and tested route of sale. We offered a 2012 Bajaj Pulsar for Rs 9,999.

Our first sale had been made. That day onwards, we droomed ahead and soon became a Rs 100-crore company.

Other investors also started showing interest. Lightbox Partners, one of the angel investors in ShopClues, had always been in constant touch with me. In May, Lightbox invested in the series-A round of funding for Droom, along with Teruhide Sato, Chaim Friedman and other investors.

IT'S DIFFERENT

Droom grew at a much quicker pace than ShopClues—largely because I had implemented the learning from ShopClues effectively.

When I started ShopClues, I was a first-time entrepreneur who was unsure of his management skills. My endurance, adaptability and decisiveness were yet to be tested.

I didn't know if I would be able to lead a company. While starting Droom, I had a better sense of what I was capable of and I also had an understanding of how to scale up a business.

There were a lot of things I did differently at Droom.

I wanted to build a company that had more to do with technology than operations. In my opinion, ShopClues was 40 per cent technology, 30 per cent retail and 30 per cent operations. I visualized Droom as 70 per cent technology, 20 per cent retail and 10 per cent operations. When ShopClues had 100 people, there were perhaps 10 engineers; Droom had 50 engineers at the time we had 100 Droomers. Right from the start, Droom was way ahead of its time in the business that it was operating. We used data science and machine learning a lot more than we ever did in ShopClues. That helped in the better prediction of customers and their preferences.

We deployed capital in a much more effective manner. Besides spending big on technology, I invested significantly in marketing. Unlike ShopClues, where we started advertising on television after more than three years, at Droom we did that after just one year.

We also scaled the business much more aggressively. A well-planned scaling up was something that was executed successfully in both ShopClues and Droom. The scaling up was aided by strong data analytics. The only difference was that I had to spend a lot more time to create the matrix for data analytics at ShopClues, whereas for Droom I spent more time analysing the data.

For example, for any department or new team or a new initiative, I customized the matrix to measure the success and plan for the future. The use of data analytics was critical to the future of Droom and I decided to bring on board some very strong data analysts.

The strategic difference between ShopClues and Droom was stark. When we started ShopClues, it was the 35th company in the e-commerce business. When Droom started it was among the very few companies in that automobile space, but none of them was our competitor. There were two online classified ad companies and five discovery platforms. All the other players in the online auto business behaved more like classified listing companies and were charging for their listings. They were no different from the advertising in the classified section of newspapers.

Droom was the only company offering a transaction platform. So, in terms of market timing, we were the category pioneers. What made us stand out was that we were out to build a platform that would generate revenue from transactions. Till then, trust was the single reason an automobile transaction between two unknown people had not been happening online. We had to ensure that there was trust between the buyer and the seller. We realized there was an opportunity to own the entire ecosystem.

We decided to focus on the two pain points for customers—trust in the condition of the vehicle and correct value of the vehicle. We created Orange Book Value (OBV) for calculating the price, Eco for inspection of the vehicle's condition, History for consolidating the vehicle historical records and Credit for consumer lending. All these different products of Droom helped in making the users trust Droom.

We created an entire ecosystem that helped both buyer and seller. The seller got the best price for their used vehicle and the buyer got the best car for their budget. Often, there would be customers who would come to our site wanting to find the price of their used car on Orange Book Value and end up selling their car through Droom and also buying their next car from us. I distinctly remember a customer who sold his old car on Droom and started looking for a used mini-SUV. He was sure in his mind that he would not be able to afford the bigger SUVs. However, he discovered a fabulous offer—a Toyota Fortuner, which was not only in great condition, but also had a very attractive price tag. What this did for us was that the price of acquiring a new customer—which can be a few thousand rupees—came down significantly.

Our marketing efforts were extremely focused and hence the spending was less. Our advertisements had a tremendous recall among customers and won us many Effies, the awards for India's best advertisements.

Another important thing I did was make sure we had more

capital than we needed at that point. Additionally, I kept scouting for new investors.

We kept building Droom on five fundamentals. The first was an extremely high sense of ownership among Droomers, who had the power and freedom to operate as 'entrepreneurs'. The second was being frugal in all our plans and initiatives. The third was to solve every problem with the help of technology and not by hiring more people. The fourth was to foster a merit-based culture within the organization. Lastly, we meticulously measured the success of every plan we ever executed.

If there's one thing Droom has taught me, it is this: 'Aim for the stars, you will definitely get the moon.'

23

COUNT YOUR BLESSINGS

A lot has changed in the Internet space since the time I started Droom, but one thing has not changed—Droom has remained a purely auto venture.

The initial vision for Droom was not just having a marketplace, but also creating an ecosystem approach. As the business grows, you need to decide your focus areas. That decision is taken based on multiple parameters—the nature of growth you want for the company, cost efficiency, monetization, but above all, you need strong economic moats. The term 'economic moats' was famously used by the legendary Warren Buffet and refers to a business's ability to maintain headway against its competition.

Like is the case with most startups, Droom also faced multiple challenges in its early days. The team was small, resources were scarce and chaos was more the norm than the exception. In all this uncertainty, I was clear about one thing—ideas with long gestation period would perhaps never see the light of the day. Hence I decided on a bunch of things that I felt would deliver faster results and power growth for Droom.

Droom was and has been a true pioneer in the auto space. There are numerous firsts to our credit among Indian startups. For example, we launched a product called 'full circle trust score'. Full circle trust score was the measuring of a seller's listing based on what is best for buyer. Droom had to be built on trust, so that was our first product. We, of course, went on to launch many other game-changing products as discussed before, like OBV, Pricing Engine, Inspection and History.

One strategy I've always adopted at every stage of building Droom is asking myself: 'How is the company placed at this point in terms of growth, cost, innovation, monetization and competitiveness?' Every decision I have taken has always been through the prism of this question.

CURSE OF A THINKER

There are multiple theories in business that tell you how to stay ahead of others. Some of these theories focus on ways to create either economic moats that will automatically lead to higher entry barriers for others or do things that will give your business a jumpstart over competitors.

In reality, however, what is critical is the speed at which you deal with the market. If you are too fast or too slow, you'll end up being at a disadvantage. If you are an obsessively original thinker, you might end up quickly creating more than what the market actually needs. On the other hand, there is also the risk of spending so much time on preparation that a competitor might end up making a better product before you. Two very good examples of business annihilation due to timing are MySpace and Hotmail. Facebook demolished MySpace and Google Mail was way better than Hotmail. I wanted to be the Facebook of my domain.

At Droom, I avoided the trap of being an excessively original thinker and also ensured there was no delay in launching products. We had no competitors in the online space as we had created something that was new but not so radical that there would be an opposition in its acceptance by the consumer.

TOYOTA LIKES DROOM

The fact that we were not just the market leaders, but also unique as well as robust in the way we grew helped us raise several rounds of funding. Since its inception, Droom has raised $123 million from nearly a dozen investors.

It was indeed a very proud moment for Droom when Toyota decided to invest in our fifth round of funding—Round D—which was also our largest round of funding till then. We managed to raise $30 million with very little dilution in equity. The trust of our investors was further demonstrated when we raised another $30 million in the next round.

The Toyota investment has an interesting story behind it.

One of Droom's early investors, Teru Sato, called me one day in January 2017 and said, 'Toyota has done global research on various automobile-focused online businesses and they seem to like Droom.' I was surprised as well as thrilled. Teru made the introductions and Toyota and Droom started chatting. In May 2017 a team of six people from Toyota flew down to India to meet us in our office in Gurgaon. They were from Toyota Tsusho, which is the trading arm of the Toyota Group, with a turnover of $60–70 billion. I had made up my mind about one thing, though—I wasn't going to sell Droom.

Fortunately, Toyota didn't intend to buy us. The initial discussions were largely on how the world of automobiles was changing rapidly, and how the offline and online businesses could come together to make the market grow even more. We also discussed how buying and selling was moving online, and why it would continue to do so, especially among millennials. Toyota wanted Droom to be a part of its digital transformation narrative. Interestingly, we also analysed how the Internet was playing a vital role in the most important decisions in a person's life. People were a click away from finding a boyfriend or a girlfriend, discovering a life partner, getting admission in a school or a university, buying a dream house, taking a loan to finance their dreams, booking a vacation, changing a job or buying a vehicle. The whole world was moving into the palms of people. The meetings with Toyota continued between May and November. After visiting India a couple of times, they invited me to Toyota's headquarters—Nagoya.

GOD LIES IN THE DETAILS

There is so much that I learnt in my dealings with Toyota. They were thorough, meticulous, detail-oriented and extremely professional. Their hard work and work ethics were amazing and their dedication was astounding. Every time they gave a presentation, their preparation was super impressive; and when we gave a presentation, they patiently went through every detail with a fine toothcomb. Another trait that is typically Japanese is the time they take to make a decision—it's painfully slow. When you are dealing with them, the slowness of decision-making might seem bothersome, but I realized this quality was their strength, not weakness. By this time I had worked with four Fortune100 companies in the US, but everything about the Japanese seemed to impress me.

I was flattered with all the attention from Toyota, but I was absolutely sure that Droom would continue to remain a brand-agnostic platform. Every car brand would be sold on Droom, including Toyota's. Hence we didn't take a lot of money from the Toyota Group. However, Toyota's ownership is symbolically important. The world's largest carmaker's investment in Droom was a huge vote of confidence in Droom and was a big bonus for my company and me.

THE LEARNING CURVE

The three most important things that I learnt from Toyota were unmatched dedication, sincerity and hard work. I also learnt that a company had to be built in a way that it would survive and thrive for a long time. The only way to do that was to have strong processes in place. Their professionalism and preparation were not different from the time we met them first till the time the funding was closed. Each person who came to the meeting had a sheet with them that had their photograph, name, designation and a short note on themselves. They would always share a proper agenda in advance before any meeting.

They always had a matrix for their proposals, where they would mention Droom's role in a particular area vis-à-vis Toyota's. They covered the minutest of details. Being an analyst, I loved their approach, but sometimes it was frustrating in terms of speed of execution. My dealing with them also taught me that startups need to have a long-term horizon when it comes to vision, but short-term when it's about the execution.

By the end of the Toyota deal, I was wiser and more meticulous. Since then, there have been many Japanese traits that have become a permanent part in the way Droom operates.

IN JAPAN, DO LIKE THE JAPANESE

It was the winter of 2017. Rishab (Droom's co-founder) and I went to Japan to meet Toyota's top management. The next day we were scheduled to travel from Tokyo to Toyota's headquarters at Nagoya. Representatives from Toyota were there at our hotel at six in the morning to take us to Nagoya on the bullet train. When I boarded the train, I thought of the numerous headlines in Indian newspapers about the bullet train idea and how fortunate I was to be sitting in one.

There were a string of meetings that day, with the final meeting being with Kashitani San, the head of Toyota Tsusho. While we discussed Droom and its plans, we ended up talking much more about technology, the future of mobility and how the online business was transforming the entire landscape of buying and selling of vehicles. Interestingly, many of the meetings had a person who translated English to Japanese and vice versa. The day ended with a dinner hosted by Kashitani San at a very traditional Japanese restaurant. We sat on the floor and had our food, much like the traditional way food is had in India.

During that trip to Japan, one of my beliefs was further vindicated—it's not as important to know English as to know how to run a company.

Once I came back to India, I got a message that Kashitani San and his team wanted to visit our office on 12 December. I was in a spot. I had to be in Zurich that very day for an event where I was scheduled to have dinner with World Bank President Dr Jim Yong Kim and Amal Clooney. Kashitani San agreed to my request of changing the date. When they finally arrived in Delhi, I decided to give them a grand Indian welcome. I thought the meeting went off very well and the synergy between the two teams was terrific.

Once they returned to Japan, they immediately sent a confirmation that Toyota was ready to invest. We signed an MOU, which basically said that Droom would expand its business to nine Southeast Asian countries—Singapore, Indonesia, Malaysia, the Philippines, Vietnam, Thailand, Myanmar, Cambodia and Laos—while Toyota Tsusho would offer the support of its relationships and dealership network, its used car inventory setup and any other physical infrastructure they had to help Droom get a jumpstart in the respective countries.

24

REDEMPTION

Freedom is like a new life—especially when all charges against you are dismissed. I can say that with certainty today, now that the US Department of Justice (DOJ) has dropped all criminal charges against me. The US SEC has also agreed to a civil settlement, entirely resolving the civil lawsuit they had filed against me.

Getting charged by the DOJ and sued by the SEC, pleading guilty with the background and information given to me at that time, and living nearly the next seven years under that cloud was not easy. For years, even while I was building ShopClues and later, Droom, I lived in the fear that one day I could be jailed, and all that I had would be gone.

My sentencing date kept getting moved further and further

ahead—which I attribute to divine power. However, the agony and the anxiety kept getting more intense. Every time a new sentencing date was announced, I was forced to relive the suspense of not knowing what was in store for me. I was afraid. Very afraid. Then suddenly one day Richard Lee, who was an accused in the same case, filed a motion to withdraw his guilty plea on the grounds that he had new evidence which showed that he had began purchasing Yahoo stocks before ever talking to me and also that his guilty plea was legally insufficient due to recent important court rulings that changed the legal community's understanding of insider trading law—including the Second Circuit Court of Appeals rulings in *US v Newman and US v Martoma,* and the US Supreme Court ruling in *US v Salmon.*

That was in August 2017, and my sentencing was scheduled for October—just two months later.

TWO YEARS OF HOPE

When Lee filed his motion, I became somewhat hopeful that the charges against me would someday be dropped. I had long and frequent discussions with my attorneys regarding this issue, and asked whether I should also file a similar motion to withdraw my own plea. After careful consideration, I decided to adopt a 'wait and see' approach. I remained confident, but still very anxious, that there would ultimately be a positive outcome.

I waited with bated breath for the judge's decision on Richard Lee's motion to withdraw his guilty plea. A week passed, then two. The date for the court's decision kept extending. Before I knew it, two years had passed. By that time, I had researched almost everything

I could lay my hands on to understand the nitty-gritty of insider trading cases.

Finally, in the third quarter of 2019, I learnt that the judge had granted Richard Lee's motion to withdraw his guilty plea, on the grounds that his plea did not satisfy all of the elements of insider trading law, as they had been clarified by courts following the date of his plea (and mine). So, instead of dropping the case against Lee, following the legal decision, the government attorneys at first indicated that they would seek to prosecute Lee at trial. Several more agonizing months passed by.

In the beginning of November 2019, the government dismissed all charges against Richard Lee. This development made me extremely happy, but I was strangely nervous. After more deliberations and discussions, my attorneys made a forceful request to the DOJ that they review my case, demanding that the charges against me should also be withdrawn.

I knew that the final outcome of this long struggle was just around the corner, but the Christmas and winter break in the US delayed the process further. The last two months were extremely exhausting.

Finally, on 13 February 2020, the DOJ withdrew all criminal charges against me. Early next week, the SEC, which had sued me in a civil case, agreed to resolve their case against me by executing a settlement agreement, according to which I agreed to pay a nominal civil penalty, among other things.

In all this while, I had forgotten what it was like to live without a legal case hanging over my head. These had been the most critical years for my sons. These were also the first six years of building Droom.

WITHDRAWING MYSELF

In hindsight, things could have turned out better if I had not been so scared about my legal case. It had become a very high-profile case for the prosecutors in the US, and it made me part from ShopClues and my family. I lost the life and the company I had built. I was too hung up in my legal case and almost withdrew from everything around me. I think I should have retained the role I had at ShopClues. I should have not let things remain uncertain and I could have taken a more holistic approach towards the case, the business and my family.

IT GOT OVER

In the last two months, before my case was finally over, I started feeling a lot less burdened. My criminal case had begun in July 2013 and based on the evidence and information provided to me by the prosecutors—as well as my understanding of insider trading law at that time—I believed that the best option for me was to plead guilty, which was what I did in November 2013. The following nearly seven years were spent in fear—the fear of having a felony record, a monetary fine and incurring possible jail time.

In these nearly seven years, I have read tons of materials on insider trading and other financial frauds. I researched thousands of cases and I learnt judges—not prosecutors—decide whether a criminal defendant should go to jail, and for how long. Although it rarely happened to those in my situation, it was always a very real possibility.

Now, more than ever, I believe that good karma and the wishes of the people who care for you does pay off.

BACK TO DROOM

Droom had a great year in 2019. It has grown rapidly—10–15 times faster than the industry growth and the GDP growth of the country. We have unbundled the entire company into six separate strategic business units.

Each of these units work like separate companies, being run by different teams, all of them reporting to me. To an outsider it seems that these are small startups, and each company has its own identity and roadmap. I want to see Droom becoming a conglomerate. For example, to build our credit business, Droom did its first ever acquisition—a banking company called Xeraphine. We also opened our operations in Thailand, Singapore and Malaysia.

We ended up clocking $1.2 billion in GMV in 2019, which was up a whopping 65 per cent over last year! In the middle of 2019, we also started fundraising for our pre-IPO round, and by 2022, we will file for an IPO and it will be listed on Nasdaq.

But some things will never change, which include me as a lifetime student of learning and the passion and values I have carried along my journey.

I'M STILL THE BOY FROM GUHLA

It still seems unreal when I look back at my life. There's much that I'm grateful for, especially for the fact that Droom is now India's largest online automobile platform.

So, what's next for Droom and me? We see robust growth

opportunities in India alone. India is the third-largest automobile market in the world, after the US and China. It's a $300-billion market, which includes sale and resale of two-wheelers and four-wheelers. Then there are opportunities in allied services such as warranty, loan, insurance, car care and detailing, roadside vehicle breakdown assistance, and much more. We expect the industry to grow and become a $400-billion market by 2025 with 5 per cent online penetration. Eve if we are able to maintain 80 per cent market share online, it would make us a $15 billion-plus company in gross merchandizing value and over $1 billion in net revenue.

There's much that this boy from Guhla is grateful for. The fact that every day is a new adventure is the biggest blessing of all.

EPILOGUE

My court battle cost me a lot more than just money and reputation—my family fell apart. Often my pillow is damp with tears when I wake up in the morning. I miss my kids. After Radhika and I got divorced, the boys have been splitting their time with both parents. While I successfully tackled every challenge life hurled at me, I have not been able to come to terms that boys and I do not live together like one family. I can still smell their presence in the house. They stay close by but it is not the same as staying together. What keeps me sane, however, is the fact that I need to keep it together for the sake of my other family—my Droom family.

As I look back, I have a sense of satisfaction because of the small contribution I have made in making India great again. In less than a decade, ShopClues and Droom have created hundreds and thousands of direct and indirect jobs, which is critical for a country like India, where job creation is the biggest challenge. I have also strived to achieve a global footprint for Droom and we are already there in many countries. While the first few steps in our foreign ventures have been taken, I am readying myself for the marathon ahead.

The acrimonious phase with Radhika is now in the past and I can safely say we are back to being friends, which is how the relationship started for us. I hope and pray that our children's lives don't get affected by our separation.

My kite needs to remain in the skies and soar higher than ever before.

IN GRATITUDE

To my mother, Savitri, who has been my guide and best friend and who taught me to be fearless, courageous and always pursue my passion.

My father, Raj Kumar Aggarwal, who made relentless efforts and sacrifices to give his family a better life. His hard work and dedication taught me so many important life lessons.

My sons, Ahaan and Arjit, who always keep me grounded. Words cannot measure the immense and unconditional love we have for each other. It was their enthusiasm to see me complete the book that kept me going. As William Wordsworth said in his poem, the child is the father of the man.

My brother, Raman Aggarwal, who has always been a like father figure, I can never thank him enough. I would not have achieved even a fraction of what I have without Raman as my elder brother. He taught me to think big, become ambitious, seek exposure, work very hard and be laser-focused in working towards my goals. He and his lovely family mean so much to me.

My sisters, Reeta and Simpy, for loving me, believing in me, teaching me to value those I love and also love myself, and adding a spiritual dimension to my life.

To Vishesh Tandon, for being my best friend and extended family. We met in 1994 and our friendship has grown immensely in these last twenty-six years. From being my counsellor to my personal cheer leader, Vishesh has done it all. I can never repay him for the way he has stood by me.

You are lucky if you have a friend like Ayushman Hazarika. I would not have come out unscathed from my legal battles if I did not have him as a rock in my life.

Amit Anand taught me the true meaning of friendship and relationships. He and his family have always been there for me.

My friends from Silicon Valley, especially Nagendra and Suruchi Shukla, Ram and Geeta Menon, Sunil and Regina Gupta, Kuntal Kotecha, Rahul Jairath and Anil Advani, have been there by my side through thick and thin over the last two decades.

My teacher Sandeep Mann for believing in me, awakening me and guiding me. He changed my life and motivated me to pursue higher education and build a career.

To Vik Mehta, a friend who helped me transition to a rewarding career on Wall Street.

To my former boss Mark Mahaney, for some exceptional learnings and experiences.

To some of my investors who are more than just investors, especially Teruhide Sato, Chaim Friedman, Itschak Friedman, Siddharth Talwar, Sandeep Murthy and Virender Rana. ShopClues and Droom would not have been possible without their undying faith in my abilities.

My team at Droom, especially Babita Vaishnawa, Shashank Sethi, Amarpreet Singh, Esha Aggarwal, Ajay Srinivas, Lipika Uniyal, Amit Kumar, Rohit Tomar, Hasmat Ali, Jhelum Sen, Abhishek Singh, Somendara Rathore, Asfak Khan, Gaurav Kumar, Mohit Ahuja, Vineeta Singh, Harshdeep Singh, Arihant Jain, Rishabh Kaila, and dozens of other team members.

My co-author Sunny Sen, whom I have known for almost a decade. He not only agreed to co-write the book but was there with me through the ups and downs. He pulled in many all-nighters even during the time when he became a father.

My editor Dibakar Ghosh at Rupa Publications, who is a rock star, full of insights and ideas, and who has become a dear friend. This book would not have been possible without his encouragement, inputs and guidance.